STEALTH BOAT

For Frank Mennel, with pleasure!

STEALTH BOAT

Fighting the Cold War in a
Fast-Attack Submarine

Gannon McHale

Naval Institute Press
Annapolis, Maryland

Naval Institute Press
291 Wood Road
Annapolis, MD 21402

Library of Congress Cataloging-in-Publication Data
McHale, Gannon.
  Stealth boat : fighting the Cold War in a fast attack submarine / Gannon McHale.
    p. cm.
  Includes bibliographical references and index.
  ISBN 978-1-59114-502-8 (alk. paper)
  1. McHale, Gannon—Anecdotes. 2. McHale, Gannon—Friends and associates.
3. United States. Navy—Submarine forces—Biography. 4. United States. Navy—
Submarine forces—History—20th century—Sources. 5. United States. Navy—Sea
life—History—20th century—Sources. 6. Sturgeon (Submarine)—History. 7. Cold
War. I. Title.
  V63.M33A3 2008
  359.9'33092—dc22
  [B]
                                    2008015587

Printed in the United States of America on acid-free paper

14 13 12 11 10   9 8 7 6 5 4 3 2
First printing

In praise of otherwise not famous men . . .
the submariners of the Cold War

First in her class, finest in the fleet!

Motto of the USS *Sturgeon*
(SSN 637)

Contents

Preface

MOST OF THIS HAPPENED over forty years ago, between March 1967 and August 1970, when I served in the U.S. naval submarine service. This book is a recollection of the men I served with and some of what we accomplished and experienced during that time. To accurately reconstruct the events in question, I visited and interviewed many of those men. They are the real authors of this book. We remember clearly not only the dangerous things we did in service to our country but also the fun we managed to have in the process, when we were younger, slimmer, faster, and smarter. Our memories are colored by the passage of time, however, and therefore must be read in the context that they are somewhat limited in scope.

This is also my remembrance of what it was like to grow up on board a nuclear-powered fast-attack Submarine. I reported on board USS *Sturgeon* (SSN 637) when I was still a boy, and I left a young man. This was the most important period in my personal development, and it profoundly affected the way I have lived the rest of my life.

The whole project began at the suggestion of my shipmate, Barry Avery, who insisted I "write down all those old sea stories." Now, there is a certain sea story element to this book, but sea stories, for the uninitiated, are anecdotal and are usually told when two or more sailors congregate for some idle time; however, they all have a modicum of truth to them, even if the embellishments often strain credulity. So even if some of what follows may seem, at times, to be fictional, that is not the case. Everything in this book actually happened, and all of the characters are not only men I served with but some of the finest men I have ever met.

The everyday working language of a submariner is, at the very least, salty, and the *Sturgeon* was no exception. By modern novel standards this language is mild, but in the interest of those who object to expletives and cursing, I have eliminated most of the ubiquitous shipboard profanity and retained only those instances that are necessary to define character or are simply too humorous to pass up.

Prologue

___

Periscope Depth, Off the Coast of Russia, Spring 1969

MY CHART SHOWED Kashin-class destroyers in two different places in the upper-right-hand corner, Osa-class torpedo boats running back and forth at high speeds across the top, and a Soviet November-class submarine smack in the middle of the quadrant while we approached from the west. The captain hung off the number 2 scope and observed everything from a distance. I had a good solution on that November class when suddenly the captain called out: "Mark these bearings. Mark! Mark! Mark! Mark! Mark! Mark!"

The captain spun the number 2 scope around and called out the bearings so quickly I couldn't keep up, and because they were as much as twenty to thirty degrees apart, they made no sense.

"This is a patrol plane flying figure eights. Just draw a big figure eight pattern around those bearings. What do we have for a solution on the target? What does 'Mr. Spock' say?"

From the analyzer at the forward end of the fire control panel, red-headed Lieutenant (jg) Hoff replied, "The increase in bearing rate indicates a course change, Captain. Contact is headed northwest, out of the area."

"What have you got, Yeoman?"

"One seven nine, five hundred yards, dead ahead, Captain."

"That's him. He's on a one eight zero course. They don't have him yet, but we do."

A moment later, the captain again called out: "Mark these bearings. Mark! Mark! Mark! Mark! Mark! Mark!" and a second figure eight pattern overlapped the first.

"Where's the 'X' in the figure eight?" the captain demanded. "Where do the lines cross? That's his target. Where's the 'X'?"

I turned toward the periscope.

"Captain . . . we're the 'X'!"

Decommissioning

A GUST OF WIND ended my daydream and brought me back to a chilly day in January 1994. The boat looked good, with her service ribbons and other decorations proudly displayed underneath her hull number, which appeared only on the inboard side of the sail. On the pier, a tent provided the guests with some shelter, but no heat. Clear, sunny, and unusually cold, the weather guaranteed a brisk pace for the ceremony. A Navy band segued from "Anchors Aweigh" to the repertoire of John Philip Sousa. I forgot about Navy protocol—when you invite flag officers to a party, the ante goes way up.

A group of middle-aged men from all over the country came to that pier in Charleston, South Carolina, to say good-bye to the USS *Sturgeon* (SSN 637), the vessel they served on some twenty-seven years earlier. Many were members of the commissioning crew, invited to the ceremony as guests of honor by the decommissioning crew. Some reported on board in the shipyard and worked twelve-hour days, seven days a week, during the boat's two years of construction, and others, like me, reported on board later for her first operational years. Also present were several former commanding officers.

The enlisted crew wore dress blues with medals, and the officers appeared in full dress with swords. An honor guard stood at attention as a boatswain's whistle piped on board the commanding officer of the USS *Sturgeon*—a commodore, four admirals (including former executive officer Bruce DeMars, the director of naval propulsion and scheduled principal speaker), and one tall man in civilian clothes.

I and almost every enlisted veteran present came not only to see the boat for one last time, but to see *him*—the one man on the dais in civilian clothes. On his introduction, every one of us instinctively stood to applaud our commanding officer, Capt. William L. Bohannan, USN (Rct.).

He began his remarks about his time on the USS *Sturgeon* with the realization that he had no sea stories to offer because almost everything we did back then was still classified.

"I'm no longer cleared to even think about it anymore," he said, "but there is one aspect of my experience on *Sturgeon* I can talk about. The thing that still stands out in my mind is the incredible confidence, dedication, and integrity of every member of the crew that I was blessed with during the four years I was entrusted with *Sturgeon*. These qualities are so prevalent in our submarine force that many of us tend to forget that the rest of the world may not be the same. During my own post-Navy experience, I have yet to find *any* team of people in the civilian world that even comes close to matching these ennobling qualities. Yes, the country is indeed blessed to have such quality folks to defend our liberty. I salute you all."

We stood only for him that day, and it did not go unnoticed.

After the ceremony, a member of the decommissioning crew came up to me and said, "We saw you guys stand for your captain."

"If you served with him, you'd have stood, too," I replied.

"He must have been good."

"The best."

The decommissioning crew member added, "And the boat was new back then."

"We were all new back then," I said.

Part I

1965–67
From Jacket and Tie to Bellbottoms

In the Beginning

I N THE FALL OF 1965, I was a "day hop" college sophomore, living in dread of midterm exams. Totally unprepared, I found myself face to face with failure. My parents, in hopes that I would be one of the "doctors, lawyers, and Indian chiefs" who ran everything in Rhode Island, made sure I attended the right schools, including St. Raphael Academy and Providence College, both of which were all-boys' schools that required students wear a jacket and tie to enter the classroom. After graduation, I was expected to pursue a conventional approach to local success, which included marriage and children and, in my case, a career in education. Teachers were in demand. A high school social studies teacher in Rhode Island could retire after twenty to thirty years in a public school system and then either start another career in a private school with less difficult students or cross the border to the neighboring state of Massachusetts to pursue yet another public school pension. The entire approach was conservative, guaranteed, and deadly dull.

After thirteen years of parochial education, I hit the wall when a priest at Providence told me that the only acceptable philosophical outlook was the *Summa Theologiae*. Though I was no philosopher in those days, even I knew there were a few other guys besides Thomas Aquinas. I wasn't enjoying college to begin with—I still lived at home and had absolutely no privacy, which made study difficult, if not impossible. A part-time job slinging hamburgers never made me enough money to go anywhere or do anything, and I spent my life going to class, work, and Army Reserve Officers' Training Corps (ROTC) drills, and then to bed in my parents' house. Miserable and facing impending academic doom, I did what anyone in my shoes would do: I quit.

Several short-lived factory jobs followed in close order, but then President Johnson escalated the war in Southeast Asia, and in early 1966, I made the next big decision of my life: I enlisted in the Navy, making a six-year commitment comprising four years of active duty and two years of inactive reserves. After a lot of thought, I considered this an acceptable alternative to facing the draft. I couldn't imagine myself surviving tours of duty in Vietnam. The recruiter—out of pity, I suspect—gave me a 120-day inactive duty deferment, which allowed me to spend the last, glorious summer of my boyhood at East Matunuck State Beach in Rhode Island. In August, armed with the greatest tan of my life, I boarded an aircraft for the very first time and headed off to Great Lakes, Illinois, for eleven weeks of basic training.

I arrived at O'Hare airport in Chicago and found myself, along with twenty or so other guys, herded into the lower level in some far corner of the terminal to wait for a Navy representative to arrive and transport us to recruit training at Naval Station Great Lakes. Hours passed before a petty officer 2nd class showed up with a bus. We arrived on the base after dark, and in a dusty old barracks with no bedding, we slept in our clothes. Hustled from one building to another for three days, our recruit company finally formed in a barracks of our own. My ROTC experience in college led to an assignment as a platoon leader.

After several weeks of training, we explored our future at a sort of job fair. We spoke to enlisted representatives from all the different parts of the Navy to see what each entailed, and in the end, each man filled out a form that listed his preferences. We called this list our "three wishes." These three preferences for your future were, of course, meaningless, as we were also told that "the needs of the Navy would always override the desires of the individual."

One sailor approached our company and asked, "Any singers here? Anyone think they're good enough for the Navy Chorus? Come sing for us. Let's see what you can do."

I sang in my church choir as a boy, and I still enjoyed singing, so I thought about it, but it wasn't for me, and the audition process itself scared me off. I wanted a real experience in the Navy: I wanted to *do* something. I wanted an adventure. I also knew I didn't want to get lost on a big command. Many of the guys in my company enlisted because they wanted or were promised a career in aviation, so they tried to get duty on an aircraft carrier. I thought that with my luck, if I went to a carrier, I would probably be relegated to the ship's laundry for four years, never to see the light of day. Then I remembered a favorite television program called *The Silent Service,* which dramatized the operational history of American submarines in World War II. So, after a short conversation with the counselor, I volunteered. Submarines were considered hazardous duty which meant receiving both sub pay and sea pay, and anything more than my $90-per-month base pay sounded good to me. At the time, I didn't realize that decision cost me any chance for an "A" school. Instead, it led to an additional set of physical and dental exams and placement on a duty roster that guaranteed I wouldn't spend time in the base galley or stand any outdoor watches during a cruel November alongside Lake Michigan.

Eight weeks of schooling at the New London Naval Base followed basic training. Submarine school included classroom work, intensive psychological and physical examinations, and pressure and escape training. Pressure training consisted of learning the Valsalva maneuver, which involves forcibly exhaling while your lips and nose are closed. This maneuver equalizes the pressure on your inner ear in situations when ambient pressure increases. If you couldn't pop your ears, you couldn't be on submarines. After we demonstrated an ability to pop our ears, half a dozen men at a time were placed inside a chamber that tested our ability to equalize down to a depth of 100 feet. For some inexplicable reason, however, once inside the chamber I couldn't get

my ears to pop. Upon completion of the test, I reported to the base infir-
mary, where they gave me some medication to help relieve the pressure.
For several hours, I thought the fillings in my teeth would explode, but
eventually my body readjusted.

Despite my inability to equalize in the chamber, the submarine
school staff cleared me for the next test, escape training in the diving
tower. While wearing a Steinke Hood—an inflatable life jacket with a
hood that completely covered my head and trapped a bubble of air—I
equalized in the escape chamber at 50 feet below the surface, then
entered the tower, placed my hands directly above me to protect my
head from coming in contact with anything on the surface, and performed a free ascent. All the way to the surface I laughed aloud like
Santa Claus, "Ho, Ho, Ho!" This technique guaranteed the exhalation of
all excess air in my lungs, which would otherwise cause the decompression sickness known as the bends. The ascent took only a few seconds,
and when I reached the surface at the top of the tower, my body flew
out of the water like a rocket. I then swam over to the ladder, climbed
out, looked directly at the instructor, and said in a loud voice, "I feel
fine, Sir," to ensure he didn't hustle me into a decompression chamber
and back down to the equivalent of 50 feet. I passed that test—one of
the most exciting things I have ever done.

Several kinds of submarines operated at that time. Squadrons of
diesel-electric–powered fleet boats made coastal patrols that often
departed on Monday and returned on Friday, but fleet boats were considered to be old—relics of World War II—and on their way out. The
real glory lay in fleet ballistic missile submarines (SSBNs): "Forty-One
for Freedom!" The core of the Navy's strategic nuclear deterrent, each
SSBN had two rotating crews—a blue crew and a gold crew—that
made three-month deployments from exotic sounding places like
Guam, Scotland, and Spain. Almost everyone in submarine school
wanted to be part of the blue-and-gold crew approach, which allowed
for a considerable amount of recreational time. I found the idea of
being at sea for months at a time doing missile drills very unappealing,

so I opted for the workhorse of the nuclear navy, fast-attack sub-marines. On graduation from submarine school, and despite my request to be assigned to the Pacific, the Navy sent me to the *Sturgeon*, which had been commissioned just nine days before my arrival. Thus, very early on the morning of March 12, 1967, I reported on board the newest boat in the Atlantic fleet.

The walk down to Pier Ten on the lower submarine base gave me my first good look at what would be my home for the next two years and ten months. Black, sinister, elegant, and huge, at 292 feet in length, the *Sturgeon* displaced over forty-five hundred tons. Ninety per-cent of the vessel lay below the waterline. Topside watch Ron Gochmonsky reported my arrival to the duty officer, and when below-decks watch IC3 Harry Heineck, greeted me at the bottom of the weapons loading hatch, I began the first great adventure of my life. I was nineteen years old.

Clueless in Connecticut

With no specialized skills and no other training except for submarine school, I found myself at the absolute bottom of the food chain on board the *Sturgeon*, and that's where COB (chief of the boat) Bill Welsh assigned me—to the galley, to serve food and clean up. Mess cooking is dreary duty, and nobody ever wants to do it. However, like every other post on the boat, it is essential. When the *Sturgeon* departed on her shake-down cruise a couple of weeks later, I occupied the unlofty position of nonqual E-3 mess cook. On board a submarine, you don't get much lower than that, and the only thing that could make it worse was to not realize it.

In the submarine service, everyone must get qualified, which means that you must learn everything about every system on the boat, pass a series of examinations given by the enlisted men who lead every divi-sion on the boat, and then pass a walk-through examination. A panel of senior qualified sailors, including one officer, conducts the walk-through. They ask critical questions along the way to determine whether you are ready to handle any emergency situation that might happen on the boat. It is all about your knowledge of systems and the safety procedures designed to ensure that, in the worst possible situation, you will do everything correctly to guarantee the safety of the boat, at a complete disregard for your own personal safety. There are scenarios in which the submariner is expected to sacrifice his own life for the remainder of the crew. The first time you pass a walk-through, you become qualified in submarines, which is a very big deal. You are presented with your dolphins—a badge depicting a submarine framed by two dolphins that is worn above the heart. It doesn't end there, though. After you earn your dolphins, you must requalify on every other boat to which you get transferred. This is a never-ending process for the submarine sailor, and each time, until you pass this examination, you remain, at the very best, suspect in the eyes of your peers. The problem with qualifying is time. You have only so much time in a day, at least eight hours (or more) of that time is spent doing the job assigned, and you do have to sleep. So, if you are a nonqual, or someone who has yet to pass the walk-through, the remainder of your free time is supposed to be spent on qualification: learn the systems, make the rounds, pass the tests, and get the signatures of the division heads.

The crew of the *Sturgeon* in the spring of 1967 featured a few young people like me and a lot more of the career sailors or lifers, some of whom had enlisted as far back as World War II. Most of the experienced guys had been in the Navy for ten to fifteen years. All of them were at least that much older than I was, and none liked what was going on in the political and social climate of the time. To many of these older, professional sailors, all young people were "hippy-dippy assholes who don't know shit," and if you appeared to fit that description, you weren't likely to get much help. I learned early on that not everyone was on my side, and my initial forays into the qualification process proved that I faced a long, difficult task.

Three cooks shared the galley responsibilities on board the boat— Jack Nelson, Norm Gilstrap, and Dick Hamilton—and I worked for all of them. As petty officers, Nelson and Gilstrap wore first-class and Hamilton second-class chevrons, and all three were career sailors. Nelson was the senior of the two first class guys, and the boss. Large, loud, bald, and tattooed from head to toe, Nelson smoked cigars, drank heavily, liked only country music, and was not particularly open to a difference of opinion. Gilstrap, who wanted to be the boss, exhibited a better sense of humor than Nelson. He also liked country music and did not tolerate a difference of opinion. Both were serviceable cooks—nothing spectacular, but reliable. Hamilton, who was a far more approachable guy, often provided the crew with undesired culinary adventures. Although he was capable of producing wonderful meals, his Yankee Pot Roast bordered on the criminal. Nelson scared me. An air of danger and irrationality hovered around him, and I never wanted to get on his bad side. However, it was Gilstrap who put me to the test.

At sea for less than a week and in transit to our first port of call, I was scrubbing pots in the galley after the noon meal one afternoon. In the middle of a hand of pinochle with some other senior enlisted men, Gilstrap yelled at me to bring him a cup of coffee. My first mistake was to even think he was kidding. My second mistake was to sass him, half-heartedly, by saying "get your own coffee." The next thing I heard was the threats.

"I gave you a direct order, boy. If you don't obey it I'll put you on report, take you to captain's mast, and fix your college boy ass."

I thought it was all a joke. When I realized he was serious, I made my third mistake: I didn't back down. His treating me like a servant did not sit well with me, and I didn't think that he had the right to do that. It got ugly—even uglier—fast. He laced into me with a series of expletives interspersed with the word "nonqual," and he was getting hotter by the minute. The next thing I knew, SD2 Emmanuel Howard cornered me in the galley. The stewards, who took care of the officers, worked in an adjacent pantry. Howard heard everything and came to my rescue. A black man who was still second class despite the fact that he had been in the Navy for over twenty years, Howard had been around the block a few times in similar situations, and the first thing he did was calm Gilstrap down. I didn't realize it at the time, but this was really serious. Howard made it painfully clear that I had absolutely no rights and that Gilstrap could make me do anything at any time, and that if I didn't do exactly what he said, Gilstrap could—and would—make my onboard life miserable. The only answer was to eat my pride, apologize in front of everyone, and bring the man his coffee. I did exactly that, and after a while it all went away. In a parental moment, a senior, experienced adult stepped in and educated a child about the reality of life on the boat.

Not really a bad guy, Gilstrap was an old school, qualified petty officer 1st class. I didn't realize it was all a test. He had baited me and pushed my buttons to see how I would respond, and I failed. It was the first of many tests that submariners do to make sure they can trust you. That's the deal. You have to be able to trust the guy next to you because he could be responsible for saving your life. It took me a long time to make up for that mistake. However, I never had any trouble with Gilstrap after that.

I learned an invaluable lesson that day. I could never thank Howard enough, but later on I did try. For the record, it wasn't just his experience in the Navy that led him to intervene—Howard had twelve children.

Emmanuel

Born in rural Lake City, South Carolina, the son of Sampson and Beulah, Howard came from a large, poor family.

"I had sisters and brothers and half sisters and half brothers. You see, my father was born in the 1800's. My grandmother, Fanny Howard, I knew her well. She was a slave. Her Master, his name was Howard. All slave owners gave the slaves their name. That's how that was."

In 1943, at the age of fifteen, Howard enlisted in the Navy: "I tried to get in 1942, but the recruiter ran me out of the office. He said 'You ain't ready yet!' You see, I didn't weigh enough. You had to weigh a hundred and twenty pounds, and I didn't weigh that much. I had to drink a lot of water and eat bananas to pass. I joined 'cause I was headed for trouble, you know. My father signed the papers because my mother wouldn't. The Navy saved me."

The U.S. Navy provided Howard with an escape from life as a poor black man in the Jim Crow South, and it gave him the opportunity to have both a distinguished career and a large family. After 29 years of service, his retirement ceremony on the submarine base was attended by family, friends, and several of the most senior and distinguished naval officers on active duty at the time. The Navy may have saved Howard, but the grandson of a slave saved me.

First Liberty

The news of my little altercation with Gilstrap spread through the boat like wildfire, and as a result, I was labeled a "big mouth and a smart ass." It was not an auspicious beginning. A few days later, we approached Norfolk, Virginia—our first port of call. Donald Deeter, a one-time 2nd class torpedoman who recently had been busted down two pay grades to seaman, and who looked like the very embodiment of Neptune himself, with longish hair, a long yellow beard, Popeye arms with anchor tattoos, and a potbelly from drinking a lot of beer, put his arm around me and said, "If you are going to have an alligator mouth, you can't have a hummingbird ass."

Loosely translated, shut up! Deeter then announced that because this was the boat's first liberty call, and my first port of call, "I'm gonna take you with me on the beach!"

Unsure whether I liked that idea, I still agreed to go ashore with him, because he couldn't be argued with.

Perhaps the most gifted man at cursing I ever have met, "Deets" was not simply colorful. He was absolutely creative about it, and he possessed a wonderful knack for interspersing a particular all-purpose expletive into the middle of another word, as though it actually belonged there. Now that talent, I suppose, showed little originality—a lot of other guys did the same thing—but no one did it better than Deets. The way it rolled off of his tongue made it sound like he invented the concept.

"Liberty is a privilege, not a right," explained the COB to all of us before we arrived in Norfolk, Virginia. A real navy town for many years, Norfolk back then bustled with activity, and all kinds of vessels tied up to the piers. With liberty call on everyone's mind, scuttlebutt ran rampant on board the boat. Deeter raved all week about a famous Norfolk bar and pool hall. He made it sound like a very important place.

"We're all going to Bell's. Everybody goes there. You're not a real crew unless you've been to Bell's. Willy Mosconi used to shoot pool in this place while he was in the Navy in World War II."

At this point, it is important to understand that Deeter was the sole source of this information. Mosconi, the former World Champion of Billiards, actually served in the Army. In any case, however, that was not my initial concern. Not old enough to legally drink, I did not want to be the kid who went to a bar and ordered a Coke. Deeter told me not to worry about anything—he would take care of that. So, on arrival at our first official port of call, we crossed the gangway and headed down the pier, past the destroyers and other such surface craft on liberty as the crew of the Navy's newest warship, the *Sturgeon*.

Located just outside of the main gate on Hampton Boulevard near the C & E piers where all the boats pulled in, stood Bell's Naval Tailors. Part of the complex included the bar and pool hall known only as Bell's. Strictly a submariner hangout, it was one of two bars, the other being the Dolphin on Granby Street in downtown Norfolk, where you could safely have a drink without getting your ass kicked. Submariners and surface craft sailors—or "skimmers"—do not get along. If you walked into the wrong bar in Norfolk, it could cost you.

I sat at the bar with Deeter. We ordered a couple of beers, and the night began. Several guys headed right for the tables, and a lot of money found its way into the jukebox. With my Gilstrap gaffe relegated to past history, the crew began to accept me. A lot of advice about how to approach my life on the boat came at me from several directions. I needed a job. I didn't have a rating, and until I could make rate, I was doomed to a life of mess cooking or work as a seaman in the deck gang, which was better than mess cooking, but not by much. I needed a profession.

All of these men were professionals: electronics technicians, electricians, enginemen, and machinist's mates—some nuclear trained and some not, fire control technicians, quartermasters, sonarmen, storekeepers, torpedomen, radiomen, and cooks. I needed to find a rate that I could do with confidence and ability, or I would never really be accepted as part of this crew. Even if I managed to get qualified, I would still need a job to remain on board. Otherwise, the Navy would ship me off to another command.

If you didn't go to "A" School after basic training to learn a specific trade, the only way you could make rate was by striking for it. To strike for a rate was difficult because you had to get someone who already had rate to sponsor you—namely, a chief petty officer or the otherwise enlisted head of your chosen division. It also required approval from the COB and the division officer. It all came down to, "What do you think you can be?" So, as I pondered my future at the bar, Deeter made sure that I held my own with the other guys. When they ordered a beer, I got one, too. It was all going along quite well until Johnnie McLean walked in.

An auxiliaryman, and an engineman by rate, McLean was one of four black men on the boat. The others included the aforementioned SD2 Emmanuel Howard, QM1 Hank Horry, and RMC P. D. Wright, all experienced, well-liked, qualified professionals. McLean sidled up to the bar and began a sly conversation with the middle-aged black woman who served us.

"Hey, baby . . . what's happening?"

She did not warm up to his overture. Her response was serious, quiet, and spoken in a voice designed to ensure the conversation would not be overheard.

"Boy, you get outta here right now. You can't be in here! Now, you go, right now."

Not about to leave, McLean ordered a beer.

"I ain't getting you no beer. You can't have no beer in here. You gotta go, right now!"

All of this transpired about two stools away, to my left, with no one in between. Suddenly, a large man about six feet two or three, well over two hundred pounds—closer to two-fifty—appeared from behind a curtain that I really hadn't noticed before then. White, nasty looking, and not friendly, he spoke to Johnnie: "What are you doin' in here, nigger? Get the hell outta here. We don't serve no niggers in here. You hear me boy? You git!"

Johnnie Mac stood five feet nine and weighed about 180 pounds. With brown skin marked by freckles across the bridge of his nose and a disarming smile, he spoke in a light, high-pitched voice that initially might give you the wrong impression. Make no mistake, though, he was no pushover. With pistons for shoulders, he was as solid as a rock and fearless. Bumping into Johnnie was like bumping into the refrigerator. Johnnie didn't move, and he didn't answer. He just stared at the guy.

I couldn't believe it. There, right in front of me, directly across the bar, was a white southern racist—a real redneck—the kind you read about in the papers. Coming from New England and taught to think along the lines of the civil rights movement, I suddenly discovered myself in the Virginia of 1967, where, obviously, certain enlightened attitudes had not permeated the world of the white working class in a Navy town like Norfolk.

Suddenly, Deeter stood just behind my left shoulder, looked at the redneck, and said, "Hey you, asshole."

Now, that got his attention, and he turned toward Deeter and me.

"Yeah," the redneck replied.

"Can you read?" Deets asked.

I thought that was a novel question to ask at that point in the conversation. Meanwhile, I was trying to get my heart, which was stuck in my throat, back into my chest. I stood a little over five feet nine and weighed maybe 150 pounds, soaking wet. Never adept at the manly art of self-defense, I found myself directly in the line of fire, and from the look in the redneck's eyes, he wasn't going over me, but through me. Desperately, I tried to be cool while the barman, somewhat confused by Deeter's query, replied, "Yeah?"

Deeter turned a little to his left and pointed to the patch sewn to the top-right shoulder of his uniform, "Well," he said, "read this."

It read USS *Sturgeon* (SSN 637). We all had one.

"Yeah . . . so what?"

Deeter smiled, and with a combination of great pleasure and quiet, yet undisguised menace said, "Count how many of 'em are in your bar, pal."

I turned my head a little to my right and noticed that everything had stopped. The pool players leaned on their cues and listened. Everyone at the bar put their drinks down and listened. At least a dozen of us, and nobody else, occupied the place. It seemed like an eternity, but I'm sure it was only a moment later when the guy behind the bar looked at Johnnie and said, "What kind of beer do you want?"

Johnnie Mac got his beer, and everything returned to normal after that. Conversations and pool games resumed, and the large man disappeared behind the curtain from whence he came and did not reappear.

Understand that Deets would never be confused with any of the great leaders of the civil rights movement: His motives had absolutely nothing to do with racial justice. This was about crew. McLean was a member of our crew, and crewmen are supposed to stick together both on and off the boat. I had signed up for attack boats because I was looking for adventure, and if that interaction was any indication of my future, I knew I had made the right decision.

Deeter got into his fair share of trouble because he always looked for it. He just really liked to scrap. In truth, Deets easily slipped out of his Navy uniform and into the black leather of the motorcycle gangs. The concept of legality was never foremost in his mind, and his biker behavior led to not only suspicions but also direct accusations of criminal activity while he was on board. In the intervening years, he spent some time as a long-term guest of the government, which is not surprising. However, none of that matters. The fact that he stood watches side by side with Johnnie McLean in the lower level of the operations compartment trumped everything. That moment in Bell's was his finest hour.

The next morning I was back to groveling as a mess cook and on duty in the galley, and I missed what transpired topside, but Bruce Kuykendall remembered for me.

"One of the amazing things about that port of call, the first stop we made, was the next morning, when we had Quarters on the pier. The only sober people were the duty section the night before. Everyone was hung over. Most of them couldn't even see straight, and [Captain] Shellman was pissed. SUBLANT (the commander of submarine forces, U.S. Atlantic fleet) came down, and Shellman asked him, 'Want to inspect the crew?' SUBLANT was an old World War II guy, and he knew what was going on. He took one look at us and said, 'That's the best looking submarine crew I've seen in years.' That whole shakedown cruise . . . that crew had been cooped up for too long."

And Norfolk was only the beginning.

Fastest Hands on the Boat!

Our next port of call was Charleston, South Carolina, where we pulled into dry dock to be sandblasted. It was the first of two times we would stop in Charleston on the shakedown cruise. The *Sturgeon* crew in 1967 was full of guys who liked to fight. Some of them went looking for fights, and others didn't have to try—the fights just came to them. Bill Drake had the topside watch one night in Charleston, and from the dry dock, he witnessed the following scene: On their way back to the boat from a night on the town, four of the younger guys, Donny Troxel, Denny Schulz, Muffy Toland, and Dick Bell, passed another submarine tied up to a neighboring pier. A few provocative words were tossed in their direction. Our guys initially chose to ignore them, but then something was said that crossed a line, and Bell turned and said, "OK, that's it! Let's go!"

Mild-mannered Schulz was the only noncombatant in this little altercation, which ended before anyone knew what hit them. According to Drake, "Schulz said . . . 'I'll hold the coats!' Troxel went down early and was kicked in the face, which put him out of the picture. That left Bell and Toland alone. The next thing you know it was over."

Bell took out two guys and told a third "you're next!" when the other side beat a hasty retreat. The next morning Troxel and Toland exhibited some reminders of the night before, but Bell didn't have a mark on him.

Richard Allen Bell was from Carson City, Nevada, and the youngest of three brothers. He joined the Navy because, as he said, "I had to get out of town!"

A typical teenager from a small, western town, Bell enjoyed himself way too much and got into way too much trouble. Finally, a justice of the peace told him "Join the service or the next time you appear here you are going to jail!"

Bell enlisted in January 1966. Submarine school in New London followed boot camp in San Diego, and despite his request for fleet boat duty in the Pacific, he reported on board the *Sturgeon* that summer with the boat still in the shipyard.

At age fifteen, Bell joined a Carson City Boxing Club that fielded two professionals, and at age sixteen he made the finals of the Nevada Golden Gloves. Simply put, he was the toughest of the young guys on the boat. Bell stood about five feet ten, with a 160-pound boxer's body, black curly hair, brown eyes, a bright smile, and a little pug nose with freckles across it that drove women crazy. It drove men crazy too. For some inexplicable reason, someone always picked a fight with him. I never knew Bell to go looking for trouble—he was the most easygoing guy on the boat—but trouble always found him, and when it did it, usually didn't last long. Years later I asked him if he thought he was the toughest guy on the boat.

"No," he said, "Johnnie McLean was the one guy I would never mess with. But if I had Herbie Youngquist at my back, I figure we could take anybody."

Youngquist, a formidable ex-logger from the Pacific Northwest, stood about five feet eight and weighed around 180 pounds, with big hands and even bigger, sloped shoulders. A nuclear-trained electrician, Youngquist shared that western, tough guy ethic with Bell; both of them were really nice guys that you just never wanted to cross. Youngquist, one of the strongest men on the boat, also had determination enough to take on the bureaucracy of the U.S. Navy and win. There will be more about that later.

Liquordale

We left Charleston and headed south to Ft. Lauderdale, Florida, for our next port. Rough weather played a big part in our arrival, and as this was the very first time that either the captain or the navigator had ever been in that particular channel, nerves were on edge. In an effort to ensure that everything would go smoothly, the line handlers were sent topside earlier than usual. With the weapons loading hatch opened, we were not prepared when a large pleasure craft passed at high speed, and its wake sent water cascading into our boat. The sonar shack flooded, soaking the equipment and ruining the rather expensive carpet that the captain had worked very hard to procure when the boat was still in the shipyard. More critical than that, the COB and two other guys were washed over the side. Attached to the boat by a lifeline for safety reasons, they hustled back on board immediately. Remarkably, no one was harmed.[1] After that, things calmed down, and with the assistance of a tug, we tied up to a civilian pier directly in front of an old British freighter.

Our arrival brought an immediate visit from the shore patrol. They came to the boat to warn us about a couple of bars in town, one of which had a really nasty bouncer who was notorious for roughing up sailors. Apparently a couple of guys had been seriously hurt. We were strongly advised against patronizing either establishment. Machinist's Mate Richard "Harvey" Tarr recalled what happened when the XO (executive officer) held Quarters on the pier: "Melton put two clubs off limits—Lenny's and the 4 O'Clock Club. As soon as he finished, he asked if there were any questions, and someone in the back said, 'Where's the 4 O'Clock Club?' Saying something was off-limits meant it was the place to go."

The morning after our arrival, the XO again held Quarters on the pier. As the COB checked the muster, he noticed that one sailor looked like he "had gotten into it with someone" the night before.

A former boatswain's mate, Armand J. Lamothe converted to quartermaster and then volunteered for and qualified in submarines. In the surface Navy, boatswain's mates are real tough guys. Lamothe wore a first-class chevrons at this point, and we referred to him as "A. J. Squared-Away." A no-nonsense, real old school sailor, he looked the part. He was always the most presentable in terms of uniform and attitude, and he didn't have to work at it. An eighteen-year veteran, Lamothe had been around the world: WestPac, the Mediterranean, he had seen it all, and he backed away from nobody.

The COB walked over to him and asked, "What happened to you?"

Bruised a bit, but otherwise all right, Lamothe smiled and replied, "That bouncer wasn't that tough!"

The British freighter tied up behind us proved to be an interesting experience. A real rust bucket, it looked like it was on its last legs. However, as our crew walked past, an invitation was extended: "Come on up!" To which we responded, "We just got in. We're going for a drink. Why would we want to board this old bucket?"

In answer came the alluring cry, "We've got beer!"

Up the gangway went several of the crew for some free beer, and once that information got around, everyone stopped in. For days, every liberty began with cocktails on board the freighter. Eventually, however, we discovered that some members of the freighter's crew were definitely "on the other team," and their intentions were more than just friendly. Once we made that determination, the party was over.

For the remainder of the week, we played the role of showboat and provided tours to politicians, local schoolchildren and their teachers, and tourists. The crew quickly tired of the tours, and when we finally left Ft. "Liquordale," we were happy to go.

St. Croix

Our next port, the island of St. Croix, provided us with fresh milk and a cornucopia of fresh fruit, both of which you run out of right away on any voyage. So as soon as we tied up, most of the crew headed off to explore what was a beautiful island on a gorgeous day in the Caribbean, while I remained on board and loaded cartons of milk and crates of fresh pineapple, oranges, lemons, mangoes, and bananas.

A bunch of guys settled into a nearby bar to drink beer and shoot pool for the rest of the afternoon. After a few hours of doing that, they set off in another direction, but STS1 John Kuester made a mistake when he decided to go off on his own in search of food. A little while later, as he walked down a street in Frederickstead, a man came from behind and attacked him. Kuester could take care of himself, and he managed to avoid the initial blow, but when the man came at him again, Kuester hit back and knocked him unconscious against the window of a shop. A policeman appeared from nowhere, and Kuester said to him, "Officer, am I glad to see you! This man came up behind me . . . "

Before he could finish, however, Kuester found himself in handcuffs, under arrest, taken to the local police station, put into a holding room, and left alone for a while. When the policeman returned, Kuester stood and asked if he could call the boat. The officer slammed him against the wall and told him to wait. A few minutes later, another policeman came in and handcuffed Kuester's hands behind his back, and then the two officers put him in a car, drove him to the local prison, dragged him into the warden's office, and roughed him up a bit. When one of them discovered that Kuester had a southern driver's license, he leaned over and said, "You're not in Georgia now, boy!"

After a while, the officers received instructions to return Kuester to the boat. At that point, another guard appeared, with a rifle in his hand, and announced, "I'll go with you to make sure this man does not try to escape."

Kuester was put in the backseat of a car, and the man with rifle sat right next to him. The driver turned to Kuester and said, "You're not going to try and escape, are you?"

Kuester replied, "Officer, I am your best friend!"

They drove him to another police station, where Kuester noticed a list of charges—and the bail associated with them—posted on the wall. Bail for murder was listed at $600; bail for Kuester's malicious mischief charge was set at $1000. COB Welsh showed up and rescued him with money from the boat's slush fund.

No one knew that some months earlier, on the neighboring island of St. Thomas, a race riot had erupted between the locals and some sailors from a visiting aircraft carrier. There was a lot of resentment on the island because of that incident and because of the way African Americans were being treated in the American South—particularly the participants in the civil rights movement. Kuester had inadvertently walked into a racial buzz saw. Weeks later, on our return to New London, we stopped in Charleston again to go into dry dock. While there, Kuester received a letter of apology from the presiding magistrate on St. Croix, and enclosed were two $500 money orders.

The other incident involving men from the *Sturgeon* on St. Croix involved Hank Marquette, Ed "Blackie" Blackford, "Salt Water" Bell, and Bruce Kuykendall—all of the A division. According to Marquette,

We're sittin' in this bar in Fredrickstead, and there were these three guys from Christianstead—on the other side of the island—and they were tied up with the Dutch chargé d'affaires. They flew in to Fredrickstead, and their plane was tied up on the beach. Blackie told them, "I know how to fly that plane." So this guy says, "You want to go for a ride?" So off Blackie went for a ride, and then he tried to fly the plane himself. He couldn't get the plane up. They kept going up and then flapping back down again, and finally Blackie crashed it on the beach and busted the landing gear! We got out of there and went back to the boat. Next morning the guy from the embassy was looking for me on the pier. I went up to meet him and he said, "You blokes all right? Just wanted to make sure that nobody got hurt."

When asked about the incident Blackie later said, "I thought I could fly it—guess I couldn't!"

Less dangerous examples of zany behavior also occurred. Dick Austin and I managed to have dinner on the island that night in an outdoor Mexican restaurant run by a couple from New England, which of course made absolutely no sense to me. I had never tried Mexican food before that night, and after Austin slyly suggested that I sample a small drop of the red sauce in the middle of the table, I couldn't taste anything for hours. Beer helped a lot, however, and we both went back to the boat feeling no pain. On the way, Austin stripped and went swimming. He walked back on board the boat wearing nothing but his skivvies.

The *Sturgeon* then went back out to sea for a couple of days, and when the captain wanted to return to dock, he was informed there was "no room at the pier." The island of St. Croix—part of the U.S. Virgin Islands, a U.S. protectorate—was not only "not protective" to John Kuester but was very happy to see the rest of us leave. We had been kicked out!

Angles and Dangles

The shakedown cruise was not just a bunch of brawls and zany escapades. We actually did do a lot of work. A shakedown cruise tests the boat and all of the equipment on it to guarantee operational readiness. You shake things down to make sure they are properly secured and do not make any excessive noise while in operation. A stealth boat, the *Sturgeon* could not afford any excess or obvious noise that might lead to our detection. We successfully performed a sea-to-sea transfer in the Bahamas, which was a difficult proposition when you consider that the boat had a rounded deck and no really flat surface to speak of. We also passed a nuclear weapons inspection in Roosevelt Roads. The boat failed the inspection back in New London because of an inability to control the line that lowered the weapon into the boat. That line had a tendency to slip while on the capstan. COB Welsh solved the problem with some submarine ingenuity. He found a way to secure the line by anchoring it to a cleat with a simple figure eight. Because that solution allowed for better control of the line, we finally passed the inspection. We also successfully shot a SUBROC missile while in the weapons testing area off St. Croix. A SUBROC was an antisubmarine nuclear rocket shot from a torpedo tube at targets within sonar range, but out of torpedo range. According to the Web site for the National Museum of American History, "the solid-fuel rocket carried a 5-Kiloton nuclear depth charge to a distance of 35 miles (56 km)."[2]

Thanks to COB Welsh, I was lucky enough to be on watch as a planesman when that shot was taken, and I remember an excited Captain Shellman tracking the missile on the periscope behind me. Welsh pulled me off mess cook duty to replace a guy named Frank McKelvey, who didn't work out in the control room. McKelvey took my place in the galley, and I got a chance to qualify as a planesman/helmsman. I never looked back. For the record, McKelvey did so much mess cook duty that year that Emmanuel Howard finally convinced him to strike for cook 3rd class, and to Frank's credit, he made it.

Shortly after the SUBROC shoot, the boat went to the Tongue of the Ocean—a six-thousand-foot-deep, one-hundred-mile-long trench off Andros Island in the Bahamas—for the maneuvering exercises known as Angles and Dangles. This is when the submarine is tested for maneuverability at high speeds all the way to test depth. The aerodynamic design of the boat made it agile and fast while submerged, and we tested her response to large rudder angles at high speeds, her ability to dive deep at high speed, and her ability to successfully get to the surface from test depth by using an emergency ballast tank blow. This procedure was an outgrowth of the SUBSAFE system installed on submarines after the loss of USS *Thresher* (SSN 593) in 1963. The valves were now an integral part of the 637 design.

We discovered that the *Sturgeon* responded to large rudder angles at high speed in a very curious way: She was definitely a "right-handed boat." Large rudder angles to port made the boat shimmy a bit, and the nose would go downward slowly. If you were not careful, she would also cavitate a bit—a very undesirable situation because the air bubbles generated by cavitation would be noisy enough to give away the boat's position. To starboard, however, large rudder angles were something else altogether. The boat responded dramatically to starboard, effectively turning the rudder into a giant stern plane. The nose headed downward at a much greater rate, with the potential of banking the boat into a spin if not checked. Knowledge of this particular design characteristic would play out comically a couple of years later.

The emergency ballast tank blow from test depth bypassed the normal ballast tank blow system, sent highly compressed air directly into the ballast tanks, and turned a 292-foot-long boat that was as tall as a three-story house into an underwater missile. With both the fairwater and the stern planes in the "full rise" position, the *Sturgeon* took on an up angle of almost 40 degrees when she breached, and a full third of the boat came out of the water. She immediately slid back down to almost 400 feet before ultimately returning to the surface. No theme park ride on the planet can replicate the sensation of that experience.

From the Bahamas we headed to Puerto Rico. One evening, while the boat traveled on the surface through a shallow area near Grand Turk Island, I found myself standing lookout on the bridge with Lt. (jg) Dennis Moritz. We witnessed the beginning of a spectacular Caribbean sunset while schools of dolphins swam alongside at incredible speeds. They jumped out of the water and across our bow, playing with us as though we were some sort of new and different, rather large whale. The sun disappeared behind purple clouds rimmed with golden arcs, while shafts of light thrust in every direction. The warmth of the evening, the colors of the water—blues and greens I had never seen before—and the unmistakable smell of the Caribbean all washed over and completely overwhelmed me. In all of my life, I have experienced only a few moments that were as beautiful.

Rosey Roads

When a boat surfaces and approaches a port, the officer of the deck sets the maneuvering watch—a special watch list made up of those men who are best at their particular watch stations plus the deck gang, who handle the lines that secure the boat to the pier. Some maneuvering watches last longer than others, depending on the size of the harbor, the approach to the port, and the degree of difficulty tying up to the pier. Bad weather, fog, tricky currents, and tides can all have a big influence, with the depth of the harbor a particular concern to us because our boat had a deep draft. None of these conditions were present when we pulled into the harbor at the Naval Air Station, Roosevelt Roads, in Puerto Rico, on a beautiful, clear, sun-drenched day, and yet it took forever to tie up to the pier. The officer of the deck, Lt. Cdr. Norman S. Elliot, was charged with bringing the boat in. The captain was supervising, and that made Mr. Elliot nervous.

A "bell" is a command from the officer of the deck or the captain to the helmsman, who relays it to maneuvering. Examples of these commands include "All ahead one third," "All stop," and "All back one third."

Officers pride themselves on how few bells it takes them to pull into a port. On this occasion, 128 bells were recorded in maneuvering, despite assistance from a tug. By the time the boat finally tied up, everyone was frustrated and unhappy. Those of us below during this ordeal went topside expecting to see a crowded harbor and a difficult berthing assignment. To everyone's amazement, we were moored to a pier all by ourselves, with no other boat activity in sight. On the other side of the pier lay an ancient minesweeper that looked like it hadn't been to sea in years. Nobody could figure out why it took so long to pull in.

Liberty commenced on arrival, but we pulled in so late that the crew missed the one bus to San Juan that left every day at noon. Of course, we were again warned—this time about certain sections of San Juan, and one street in particular. Harvey Tarr remembers that "They told us one side of the street had a native market and the other had bars and cathouses. The native market was off limits. Go figure."

The chiefs' club on the base was open, and the goat locker emptied its chief petty officers in that direction. The officers' club was open, and that's where the inhabitants of the wardroom headed. The captain and the XO also were to spend the night ashore, leaving only one officer on board with the duty, Lt. (jg.) Richard Shreve. The tall, handsome, easygoing reactor officer (we called him "Reactor Rick") cut a dashing figure as he drove around the New London submarine base in his XKE Jaguar. Later that evening, he came topside in a T-shirt and fished off the stern of the boat.

The enlisted men's club, however, was closed. As a consequence, most of the crew had no place to go because the towns surrounding the base were also off-limits. That didn't stop some guys from sharing a cab to San Juan, which was miles away, and others from disregarding the warnings and venturing into forbidden territory. Most of us, however, stayed on the pier, and that's where things got really crazy.

I went topside early in the evening. A few guys lounged around as an ice cream truck made its way down the pier. The driver rang a bell and yelled in a heavy Spanish accent, "Ice Cream! Ice Cream!"

Deeter made it clear, as only he could, that we had no interest in ice cream.

"No, ice cream . . . ice cream!" continued the driver, and he beckoned Deeter and me over to the truck. When we got to the back of the truck, he showed us a few boxes of popsicles on top that lifted to reveal several cases of beer underneath, which he was willing to sell to us at fifty cents a can.

"OK, we'll buy *that* ice cream!"

And so the night began. The ice cream vendor came and went several times to keep us supplied. We drank beer, listened to sea stories, and enjoyed a gorgeous evening in the tropics. Around midnight, the real entertainment began as the crew staggered back on board in various states of inebriation.

The chiefs returned first, feeling no pain at all, and HMCS Woodrow "Doc" Reed decided to go swimming, fully clothed. STC Ted Lee produced a bottle of 151 rum and joined the party on the pier. Meanwhile, EN1 Stephen William "Salt Water" Bell took up residence atop the telephone booth at the head of the pier. One of the smartest guys on the boat, Bell was also one of the more eccentric. Rail thin and covered in tattoos, he sported a pronounced beer belly and was given to expounding at length on any subject at any time. His stomach featured the most celebrated piece of his body art: a smiling cartoon bunny rabbit that looked back at you while it headed in the other direction. Strategically placed, it allowed Bell's belly button to embody the back end of the rabbit's anatomy. From the lotus position atop the phone booth, Bell conducted a rambling, incoherent monologue interrupted only when he spat at passersby who came too close. No one was sure where he had been that night, or what he had been drinking, but he claimed aloud that he could spit better than anyone on board, and to prove it he would demonstrate the "parabolic arc of a Polaris Missile." At that point, Deeter said, "He must've been into the Gilly!"

Gilly, the 100 percent, not denatured, alcohol used to clean the heads of tape recorders and other sophisticated electronic gear on board, became a particularly potent cocktail when mixed with orange juice. However, too much Gilly could cause brain damage, and Bell, truthfully, did not need any help in that area.

On their return, it was the officers, however, who provided the evening's true comic relief. A couple of them almost fell overboard as they made more than one approach to the gangway, and their attempts to maintain some sense of dignity proved hysterical. Navigator George Davis apparently found it too warm to sleep below, and he reappeared topside only a few moments after he returned and promptly went to sleep a couple of yards aft of the weapons loading hatch.

Then the real fun began. We looked toward the end of the pier and saw Muffy Toland weaving his way toward the boat. He dodged the parabolas of expectorate hurled at him by Bell, and the two of them exchanged a series of expletives. Instead of joining us, however, Muffy went directly below. Not ten minutes later, we heard the siren. At the time, we didn't know that Muffy had gone to visit one of the towns that were off-limits, and when he returned, he had an altercation with a Marine who was on guard. So we were amused when a jeep with no fewer than three Marines came roaring down the pier, looking for Toland. One drove, and the other two stood as they held on to the roll bar. All three wore pistols. The jeep stopped alongside the boat, and the two Marines took positions on either side of the gangway while the driver walked on board toward our topside watch, who, as fate would have it, was the perfect person for this situation: Ronald P. Gochmonsky of Clifton, New Jersey. Known to all as "Dimmerswitch" or "Goch," he possessed the most laissez faire attitude on board. The Marine looked at Goch and said, "I want to speak with one of your officers."

Goch looked aft, saw Rick Shreve as he fished off the stern and George Davis asleep a few feet away. He looked back at the Marine and said, "Well, there's a couple. Take your pick."

The Marine outranked Goch and demanded to see the duty chief. RMC Don Zingrich came topside, and when the Marine repeated his demand, "Zing" looked around and said, "Well, there's one right over there. Why don't you go over and wake him up?"

The Marine, aware that Zing outranked him, threw his hands in the air. The three Marines got back in the jeep and drove away to a round of applause from our crew on the pier. They never came back.

We remained in Puerto Rico for a week. I managed to take a trip to San Juan for a day, where Dick Austin and I caught all the tourist sites, including El Morro Castle and a few others that would never be found on the typical tourist brochure. Meanwhile, thanks to the ice cream man, the nightly party on the pier continued.

Toward the end of the week, a realization began to form. Because we were at a naval air station, a statement had to be made—something had to be done before our departure. There was a large water tower on the base, but the base commander had made it clear he wanted no incidents involving drunken submariners trying to inscribe their boat's numbers on his recently painted tower. Captain Shellman also made that clear when he told everyone to "lay off," yet, despite the warning against pranks of any kind, two unlikely culprits from the wardroom remained undeterred. Armed with a set of wire cutters, lieutenants Shreve and Davis broke into the officers' club on the base one night. They stole a large set of gold pilot's wings, which were mounted on the wall for decoration, and brought their trophy back to the *Sturgeon* wardroom. Captain Shellman, on seeing the wings the next morning, was somewhat amused. XO Melton, however, was not and insisted that Davis and Shreve return their prize immediately. They agreed to do so, but before they did, they made a slight modification: They attached a couple of sets of gold submariner's dolphins onto the wings and then remounted them on the wall of the officer's club without being discovered.

Melton remained upset, however. He lectured the chiefs and officers about setting a bad example and openly complained that the crew was ruining the boat's reputation. It almost goes without saying that the crew saw things differently. Still, rumor had it that when we left, our departure from Rosey Roads had once again been requested.

Ichabod

The commissioning crew XO, Lt. Cdr. Wade I. Melton, a dark-haired, gaunt, deeply religious man, often proselytized on the 1MC (the communications system heard throughout the boat) when quarters were held on station. When COB Bill Welsh went to Captain Shellman to explain that not everyone on the boat had the same religious convictions, Melton agreed to compromise and resorted to quoting scripture in the plan of the day. Charlie Perry, a rotund Forward IC whom we suspected to be the son of a preacher, would find alternative, salacious verses from the Bible, and when there were no officers around, he would scribble them in red just below Melton's selection on the plan of the day in the crew's mess. It drove Melton to distraction when he couldn't find out who did it.

When Melton worked in his office, he kept a little bell on his desk that he rang to summon his yeoman. The yeoman did not appreciate that, and when word of this practice got out, everyone on board ridiculed it by saying things like "I'm gonna ring your bell!" or "Don't ring my bell!" and the worst of those was "I'd like to ring the XO's bell!"

As XO, Melton was responsible for discipline on the boat, and his approach was as stern as his appearance. A pious Christian, he was offended by bad language, which meant that on our boat he was offended most of the time. Auxiliary Chief Hank Marquette rang the XO's bell more than once, and if not for COB Welsh, he would have lost his chief's hat, especially after he and Blackford got drunk in Elfie's bar one weekend while the boat was still in the shipyard and decided on the spur of the moment to fly to Duluth, Minnesota, for a cocktail. Once there, they had no hope of making it back to Connecticut in time for quarters on Monday morning. They were missing for a couple of days, but amazingly, Welsh managed to keep them both from being busted.

As a result of this contentious relationship, Marquette irreverently referred to Melton as Ichabod because of his resemblance to the character in *The Legend of Sleepy Hollow*. As described by Washington Irving, "He was tall, but exceedingly lank, with narrow shoulders, long arms and legs, hands that dangled a mile out of his sleeves, feet that might have served for shovels, and his whole frame most loosely hung together."[3]

The nickname stuck. However, when the *Sturgeon* returned to the submarine base in the summer of 1967, change would be the order of the day when Ichabod's relief reported on board.

Muffy

After Puerto Rico, we returned to Charleston, South Carolina, and tied up alongside the submarine tender, which put anyone who wanted to go on liberty at the mercy of the submarine tender's duty officer. Now, duty on a submarine is, by nature, not as disciplined as life on a surface craft, and as I discovered in Norfolk, skimmers—any sailors who serve on board a surface ship—and boat sailors (submariners) do not get along together. So almost immediately there was tension. Several guys from our boat were denied liberty because their uniforms were not up to the standards of the submarine tender. Some needed a new white hat, or their shoes weren't polished, or the duty officer just didn't like them and sent them back until they got squared away; in every instance, this interference was not appreciated. Sometimes, however, what goes around comes around, and in this case what came back around was Muffy Toland.

The only other guy on the boat who rivaled Deeter in the ability to curse was his partner in the torpedo room, TM2 Thomas A. Toland. Toland was one of the boat's divers, and as such, he was immediately given the nickname "Muffy," which for the uninitiated is a blatant sexual reference. Toland stood about five feet seven, with a muscled body and no fear—he was as tough as nails. Very high strung, Toland suffered from a short fuse that often got him into trouble. He stuttered a bit, and when he did, he would curse just to get himself going. He also spoke very quickly. In fact, he spoke so fast that it was difficult to understand what he was saying. The end result was that I never heard him say anything without cursing, and because of the stuttering, his sentences often began and sometimes ended with an expletive. This problem was so pronounced that COB Bill Welsh called him "Brrrrrupfuck," and when he did . . . well, you can imagine the response! I know it sounds silly, but forty years later, it still makes me laugh.

Located amidships, in the lower level of the three-tiered operations compartment, lay the torpedo room. When we loaded weapons, we had to remove the first two decks, and the "fish" passed by the XO's stateroom, the captain's stateroom, and the galley, which meant that anything said in the torpedo room was in earshot of the entire operations compartment, and when Deeter and Toland worked together, their conversation was nothing less than an barrage of expletives interspersed with threats of bodily harm and punctuated by the sounds of wrenches—often thrown at one man by the other. It was a profane *Katzenjammer Kids* cartoon, only in the torpedo room, and it drove the XO crazy. Toland's other significant personality trait was a pathological dislike for the U.S. Marines.

We were in Charleston for maybe a day before Muffy got himself into a jam. He came back from liberty one night crocked and walked up the first gangway he saw—onto the quarterdeck of the tender. In his condition, he also failed to notice that the first gangway was reserved for officers. He was stopped by the tender's duty watch, some strong words were exchanged, and Muffy was put on report. The charges against him were serious enough that the commanding officer of the tender insisted that the captain's mast—nonjudicial punishment—be held on the tender. Our captain agreed, and Muffy was restricted to our boat until the captain's mast could be scheduled. He was sure to get busted, and everybody knew it—including Toland.

Then a very unfortunate incident happened. One of the crew members of the submarine tender came back from liberty intoxicated. He fell into the water between the ship and the pier and drowned. For some reason, there were no divers available to search for the body, which put the captain of the submarine tender in a very difficult position. Even a search and rescue boat assigned to the task failed. A request came to the *Sturgeon* to use our divers. So Muffy donned his gear and, along with our other diver, Mike Helms, went over the side in search of the body. After twenty minutes, Toland surfaced, spat out his mouthpiece, and yelled nervously at the rescue boat, "Get him off me!" The drowned sailor had apparently hit his head on the way down, and Muffy found him on the bottom, but the drag line was wrapped around both Toland and the corpse, and that made Muffy uncomfortable. The search and rescue boat hauled the body of the dead sailor on board, and the commanding officer of the tender expressed his gratitude by dropping the charges against Toland.

The next night, Muffy headed off on liberty again. He came back feeling absolutely no pain and deliberately walked up the officers' gangway to the quarterdeck of the submarine tender. Stopped by the same two guys who put him on report, Muffy stood there while they looked at him and asked, "Where do you think you're going?"

"Back to my boat," Muffy replied, "You don't like it? Call your captain."

At that point, the officer of the deck walked over and asked, "Are you the diver?"

"Yep," Muffy replied.

"Let him go," the officer said, and with a big smile, Muffy strolled past the two skimmers on duty, across the quarterdeck, and back to our boat.

Changes in Latitudes and Attitudes

The *Sturgeon* surfaced in the Narragansett Bay operations area on July 15, and the first thing the mess cooks did was turn on the radio in the crew's mess. Young men love their music, and WABC in New York was the king of the AM Top-40 radio stations. The line handlers gathered in the crew's mess to listen to the latest hits while playing furious games of cribbage and pitch as they waited to go topside to tie the boat up. Everyone was anxious to get back home and see their wives and girl-friends.

Denny Schulz was headed home to Cleveland for a week of leave on arrival. He took his leave chit and went in search of the duty officer, Lieutenant Davis, who was required to sign off on it. Davis always took the first night's duty on arrival. No explanation was offered—it was just something he did.

Schulz found him in the control room. Davis looked at him and said, "Do you have a pen?"

"No, sir. I don't," replied Schultz.

"Well, Schulz you are in violation of the seven-'Ps' rule. 'Prior proper planning prevents piss-poor performance'!"

Davis found a pen and signed the chit and Schulz, replete with a memorable aphorism, finally got to go home.

After being away for almost five months, we had much to catch up on. A record album called *Sgt. Pepper's Lonely Hearts Club Band* by the Beatles—the biggest musical group in the world—topped the charts. It held the number one position for twenty-seven weeks in Britain and for nineteen weeks in America. Other albums released that summer included *The Doors*, the Jefferson Airplane's *Surrealistic Pillow*, and Cream's *Disraeli Gears*—all of which were destined to be rock music classics.

On the international front, Israel fought the Six-Day War against Syria and captured the Golan Heights, the Gaza Strip, the West Bank, and East Jerusalem.

In America, civil unrest dominated the national news. Race riots erupted in New Jersey, North Carolina, Wisconsin, Tennessee, and Michigan. The worst rioting happened in Detroit, where forty people died, two thousand were injured, and five thousand were left homeless. President Johnson dispatched forty-five hundred paratroopers to put an end to the rioting, burning, and looting that went on for days.

The Supreme Court struck down state laws prohibiting interracial marriages, and President Johnson nominated Thurgood Marshall to become the first black justice on the U.S. Supreme Court. Marshall, a leading civil rights lawyer, argued the landmark *Brown vs. the Board of Education, Topeka* case in the Supreme Court and served as U.S. solicitor general. His tenure on the court lasted until 1991.

Gen. William Westmoreland claimed he was winning the war in Vietnam but needed more men. In response, President Johnson announced plans to send 45,000 more troops to Vietnam. Some things never change.

Sidney Poitier, the country's biggest box office attraction, starred in such movies as *In the Heat of the Night, Guess Who's Coming to Dinner*, and *To Sir with Love*. Other popular movies that year included *The Graduate, Cool Hand Luke, Bonnie and Clyde, In Cold Blood*, and *The Dirty Dozen.*

Psychedelic, the adjective of the moment, described much of what happened in San Francisco during "the Summer of Love." Meanwhile, tied to Pier Ten in Groton, the *Sturgeon* readied for her first deployment.

The new XO, Lt. Cdr. Bruce DeMars, came from Chicago. A polished Naval Academy graduate, his prior experience included service on board the attack transports USS *Telfair* and USS *Okanogan*. After submarine school, he served on board the *Captaine* (SS 366), *George Washington* (SSBN 598), and *Snook* (SSN 592). He reported on board the *Sturgeon* after attending the Armed Forces Staff College. Shorter in stature and much more pleasant and approachable than Melton, DeMars also exhibited a sense of humor. Thoroughly professional, he proved to be tough but fair as XO. Obviously on the fast track to command, he had a unique gift. No matter what, he was always the smartest guy in the room: You just knew it.

Change was immediate. To widespread approval from the crew, a daily movie listing replaced the quote from scripture. A number of personnel changes also happened. Men who reported on board at the beginning of the boat's construction period transferred off, and new men arrived as the *Sturgeon* prepared for her first extended deployment. Overall, the crew became younger and, with a couple of notable exceptions such as Charlie Perry, leaner. Widespread speculation existed about a "northern run," the submarine euphemism for a patrol. From that point forward, the *Sturgeon* would spend more time in the seldom-friendly confines of the North Atlantic.

At the onset of the shakedown cruise, I mess cooked. Up to my ears in potatoes, I peeled them, washed them, cooked them, mashed them, ate them, and cleaned them out of the trash compactor—a truly awful job. As a kid from an Irish-American background, I was grateful when we served rice. At the end of the cruise, the COB assigned me to the deck gang. All my attempts to find a job failed. I thought I might be good at charts, but the quartermaster chief soundly rejected me when I asked to strike for that rate. My buddy Dick Austin had storekeeper covered, and radio, which my boot camp counselor had advised, had no room. Not mechanically inclined, and with electronics way beyond my comprehension, I ran out of options. Then my salvation appeared in the form of YN1 Hanson Alva Slack.

Compared with the collection of bruisers and brawlers that populated our crew, "Tim" Slack was at the opposite end of the personality spectrum. A mild-mannered, bespectacled, soft-spoken, quiet, happily married guy with a subtle sense of humor, Tim reported on board the *Sturgeon* in the shipyard before she was built. The incredibly efficient right-hand man to the XO, Slack occupied one of the most important positions on the boat. An old Navy axiom held that "you don't mess with the cook, the corpsman, the yeoman, or the storekeeper." Every piece of correspondence that originated on the boat or came to the boat passed through his hands. He also maintained the service records of every man on board, which was the real reason you never messed with the yeoman. The billet on the *Sturgeon* called for two yeoman, a first class and a third class, or a chief and a striker. Slack's partner, Bob Bristol, made second class and was scheduled to be transferred. Tim looked forward to the chiefs' examination, and all of that added up to an opening for me.

Everyone on board stands watch underway, and the COB had already assigned me to planesman/helmsman watches in the control room for the upcoming deployment. Apparently, I did pretty well during the SUBROC shoot and in the Tongue of the Ocean. Slack then approached me and suggested that while we were at sea, and as long as he was not working on the patrol report, I could use some of my time off watch to work in the yeoman's office as his assistant. He would teach me everything he could, and with work, I would be eligible to take the examination for third class in the winter. The COB wasn't thrilled with this idea, because he would lose a member of the seaman gang, but DeMars' approval tipped the scales in my favor. It was a real break, and I grabbed it.

The first thing I had to do was learn how to type. If I couldn't pass the typing test, the opportunity would go away. That summer, I spent most of my off time at work in the office and at the typewriter. Fortunately, there were manuals, and Tim Slack was supportive, helpful, patient, and kind. When the time came, I passed the typing test and officially became a yeoman striker.

The Legend of Randy Little

Escape from mess cooking brought with it a change of address on board. Up until that point, I had been living with the cooks in crew's berthing Charlie, which was located on the middle level of the operations compartment. Now I found myself assigned to a rack inboard of a torpedo tube in crew's berthing Delta. This collection of bunks just forward of the fire control panel in the torpedo room on the starboard side of the boat was my home for over a year. Delta housed the younger guys on the boat: Denny Schulz, Bill Drake, Dick Austin, Barry Avery, Dan Albright, Gary Cornibert, and others all lived there at one time or another, but one man stood apart from all the rest.

In the rack directly above mine in Delta slept one of the unique personalities on the boat, Randy Little. An Oklahoma boy, Little was a tall, blond, pious Christian with pronounced ears. Officially a forward electrician, in reality he played the role of the boat's often maddening, yet still lovable, resident doofus. If the entire crew of the *Sturgeon* suddenly morphed into Walt Disney characters, Little would be Goofy.

My first exposure to the always-entertaining Little happened on a summer evening in 1967. Back from the shakedown cruise and ensconced at Pier Ten North on the submarine base, I assumed the 2000–2400 topside watch on a glorious night. Thirty minutes later, my enjoyment of the beauty and stillness of the river; the unmistakable smell of the submarine base—a combination of metal, saltwater, and diesel oil; and the last quiet, peaceful hours of daylight all exploded into bits with the sound of the collision alarm. Stunned for the moment, I tried to figure out what happened. With the boat tied to the pier, the topside watch controlled the collision alarm, and yet without any input from me, it rang out loud enough to draw the attention of the neighboring boats. The only "close aboard" threat, a family of ducks, paddled past on the outboard side. Suddenly, the duty officer, Lt. John C. Brons, who was also the boat's engineer, stuck his head up the weapons loading hatch and said, "WHAT!!!!"

I don't know if it was the way he said it or the inanity of the situation, but I really had to work hard to suppress a laugh at that moment. When I pointed to the ducks, he muttered something indecipherable and disappeared below. After a few minutes, we secured from the alarm. I would later find out that below decks watch Bruce Kuykendall discovered the ever-inquisitive Little at the fuse panel in the after end of the torpedo room. One by one, Little examined each fuse to see what it looked like.

"Gol-ly . . . look at that!" Kuykendall reported Little as saying. Kuykendall then said, "What are you doing?" Little replied, "Checking these fuses." To which Kuykendall answered: "PUT THE FUSE BACK!"

Kuykendall later told me, "I could have killed him right then and there!"

Sleeping quarters on board the *Sturgeon* were, as in any other submarine, cramped. Individual storage consisted of a shallow tray underneath your mattress, which easily filled up with clothing and other necessities. Despite this limitation, Little managed to have the most amazing collection of nonessential stuff on the boat. We slept on the outboard side, where pop panels allowed access to the inboard side of the torpedo tubes right next to us. Little would open those panels and store things in there, which drove the torpedomen crazy. He seemed to have a need for stuff that he could never possibly use while the boat was underway on a long operation: fishing tackle, swim fins, goggles, a snorkel, and a lot more. Bill Drake said, "I think he had every possession he owned in that rack! I don't know how he managed to get any sleep up there!"

One day, with the boat underway, I lay in my rack and read a book to put myself to sleep after a six-hour watch on the planes. Little came into the compartment, and when he noticed I was awake, he asked me, "Hey Mac, have you seen m' sword?"

I really couldn't believe what I heard. In his bunk across the way, Austin giggled at the absurdity of the question. "Randy," I replied, "I know you've got a lot of stuff up there in that rack of yours, but a sword? What kind of a sword? And what are you doing with a sword on a submarine in the first place?"

Bill Drake walked into the middle of this conversation, and we all completely lost it when Little replied, "Oh Mac, it's not a real sword, it's m' Bible!"

Goofy or not, you had to love him.

On another occasion, during the preparation for an upcoming patrol, Chief Hank Marquette sat in the control room and tested the hydraulics for all of the masts. He raised each mast all the way up and then all the way back down again. A check of the indicator lights on the ballast control panel assured him that everything was in order. For some reason, the electronics countermeasures (ECM) mast would not register as down, or "faired." The largest and heaviest of the masts in the sail, and chock a block full of sophisticated sensors for the clandestine monitoring and analyzing of another vessel's communications equipment, the ECM mast was a very expensive piece of gear.

In my office, I could hear Marquette swearing in the control room. The mast would go up and then slam back down with such force that you could feel it throughout the boat. Each time, that sequence would be followed by a string of expletives. This happened repeatedly for about fifteen minutes. From a distance, it was very entertaining, but Marquette was more than a little upset. He finally went down to crew's berthing Delta to check the ECM mast well, which was behind a panel that sat deck level between my rack and Austin's. When Marquette opened that panel, he discovered what was left of a trumpet—Randy Little's trumpet. Like an image from some cartoon, it had been completely flattened to the point where it was useless. Later, when Marquette found Little in the crew's mess, he almost had to be restrained.

We lived on an ultraquiet vessel designed to travel submerged and to never be discovered. When and where Little thought he could practice the trumpet remains a mystery to this day.

Goin' North!

In the late 1960s, the Soviet naval submarine force outnumbered that of the United States by more than two to one, but America enjoyed the advantage of having more nuclear-powered subs and better technology. Russian boats were noisier, couldn't go as deep, and were easier to detect. The Soviets tried to improve, however, and they added to their nuclear fleet at a rate of five boats per year.

The submarine strategy for the Cold War centered on the fleet ballistic missile submarine (or SSBN) as a mobile nuclear weapons launching platform that could operate from any point in the world's oceans in complete secrecy. The boomers, as the submarines, and the men on them, were known, would go to sea and find a strategic hole in the ocean where they could remain undetected for months. Most of the Soviet submarines were hunter-killers designed to find the American SSBNs. However, the Soviets also built subs with missile capabilities, and part of our mission as a fast-attack boat was to hunt those missile subs, get behind them, and, in the case of a real wartime situation, sink them before they could launch. Attack submarines also gathered information about any new subs being built by the Soviets. To do that, we traveled to where the new subs made their first appearance—somewhere off the coast of Northern Russia. Murmansk was home port for the Russian Northern Fleet, and it was their only deepwater port on the eastern end of the European continent. American submarines would transit to a designated point and just wait for the Soviet submarines to come out of the barn.

A submarine's weakest point lies directly behind it. The screw that propels the boat forward churns the water directly behind it and creates a disturbance known as the baffles, which prevents the sonarmen from hearing anything in this baffle area. So a boat has to clear the baffles occasionally to make sure that no one is following. American boats did this on a regular basis by altering course to allow a brief sweep of the area by sonar before returning to base course. Performing this task at different times and in different directions ensured that no traceable pattern developed. The Soviets, in contrast, acted in an unpredictable manner when they suspected someone was behind them. Known for a maneuver called a Crazy Ivan, the Soviets would attempt to get behind their pursuer with an abrupt course change at high speed, which often resulted in a game of underwater chicken. Collision in these instances was a very real possibility.

A stealth boat, the *Sturgeon* sacrificed the speed of earlier classes of submarines for a distinct advantage. Still very fast, she was ultraquiet and, with advanced sonar technology, perfectly designed to detect Soviet submarines at long range. She could then approach from behind and, when close enough, record the Soviet vessel's sound signature. An acoustic fingerprint, that signature comprised the total of the submarine's sounds, including the propellers, any noise from machinery on board, and the character of its wake. After the fish, whales, and other biologicals were filtered out of the equation, the details of that submarine's signature would be further analyzed by some guys in Washington who had even better ears than our sonarmen. By recording all the vessels in the Soviet submarine fleet, it would be easier for other American submarines to identify particular boats in the future. If we could identify all the Soviet missile boats, we would be able to track them at every moment, and if there were enough American attack submarines to get behind every Soviet missile submarine, then the Russian attempt at nuclear missile parity at sea would be nullified. This theory called for a submarine captain who was comfortable with aggressive tactics and who was also willing to take a certain amount of risk. As we headed north on our first special operation, we were unaware that our captain did not fit that description.

Charlie Tuna

Cdr. E. A. Burkhalter was originally named to command the *Sturgeon* in the shipyard, but he was reassigned to USS *Skate* (SSN 578). The Navy's second choice, the son of a former chief quartermaster, would go on to become, according to Rear Adm. George Davis, "The finest boat builder in the Navy."

Cdr. Curtis B. Shellman grew up in New London and attended Chapman Tech, where, according to Leo Facchini, the current athletic director at New London High School, Shellman was "quite a track star, consistently winning the 100-yard and 220-yard dashes."

In 1948, Shellman set a record in the 220-yard dash in a track meet against Billard Academy. He graduated from the Naval Academy in 1952. Before the *Sturgeon*, he served on board USS *Entemedor* (SS 340), went around the world submerged on board USS *Triton* (SSN 586), and did a tour as XO on board USS *James Madison* (SSBN 627). On the day that he assumed command, Shellman called COB Welsh into his office and told him, "You only have to work half a day, six in the morning until six at night, seven days a week."

That was the work schedule for the wardroom and most of the crew for the following two years. Lt. George T. "Skip" Borst, the supply officer during the construction period, said, "Shellman had his fingerprints on every bolt, every screw, and every piece of equipment on that boat."

Known to all as "Pop" Shellman, his father worked for the Shipyard Test Organization. Although not an engineer, Pop Shellman was connected enough in the yard to know what was right and what was not. He stood the graveyard watch and would often show up in the captain's office in the morning and say, "Come with me."

He would then take his son down to the boat and point out something that was inadequate and say, "Do you see that? That's not right. Don't let them get away with that."

Captain Shellman became a stickler for details and thus began a contentious relationship with the shipyard workers that would last for over twenty years.

Borst said, "He did manage to do one thing that nobody had ever done. He managed to break down the wall at EB [General Dynamics, Electric Boat Division] on spare parts. When *Sturgeon* was complete, we had all of the spare parts that we needed on board, and that had never happened in the shipyard before."

Years later, Bruce DeMars told me that "We had two of everything!"

COB Welsh said that the keel for the *Sturgeon* lay fallow for two years between 1963 and 1965 while EB worked overtime to deliver the SSBNs under construction at the same time. As the new captain of the boat, Shellman marked all requests for the *Sturgeon* as priority, in the same manner as the SSBNs. The shipyard supply people did not differentiate between the SSBNs and the *Sturgeon* as an attack sub. As a result, the boat received two of everything.

For two years in the shipyard, Shellman successfully supervised the construction of the lead boat—the first in a class of thirty-seven submarines that served as a vanguard in the nation's Cold War struggle against the Soviet Union for over twenty years. In twenty-seven years of operation, the *Sturgeon* steamed three quarters of a million miles, which is equal to going around the world thirty times—and 90 percent of that submerged. During that period of service, no major structural failure was ever recorded.

However, in 1967, when the boat became operational, Shellman's temperament seemed to be at odds with the nature of the vessel he commanded. Outwardly he appeared a serious, somewhat dour, humorless personality who seldom smiled. Storekeeper Mac McCollum recalls that he "saw him smile four times in two and half years."

In truth, Shellman was a quiet, shy man, whose physical demeanor belied what went on inside him. Lt. Richard Shreve said, "His face in repose, unfortunately, gave one the idea that he was always unhappy."

With dark circles and bags under his eyes from a lack of sleep, he chain-smoked long green cigars, often keeping one dangling from his lip. He did not wear clothes well. The shape of his body made him appear sedentary, and despite his history of high school athletic prowess, he moved without a sense of agility. The overall effect made him somewhat unattractive.

Navigator George Davis said that it took some time for him to get to know Shellman, but once he did, everything was fine: "He loved to go to parties. You would never know that if you looked at him, but he did. Unfortunately, when he was at the party he always looked like he wasn't having a good time, when in fact, he was!"

A cautious operational commander, Shellman's character perfectly suited the command requirements of an SSBN—not a fast attack. It would be this sense of caution, more than anything else, that would make him unpopular with his crew in the fall of 1967.

After two weeks of submerged transit in early October, we arrived at our designated operations area with orders to remain on station for thirty days before we could head home. Because we were so far north, we lost minutes of daylight every day, and as soon as we arrived, the weather turned for the worse.

At three hundred feet or more, depth control for a submarine was a matter of the diving officer keeping the boat in trim and of doing some fine tuning with the stern planes. We negated any storm or bad weather on the surface by going deep, which kept the boat quiet and allowed the sonarmen to listen for contacts. Depth control at periscope depth was much more difficult, and from time to time, we had to come shallow so the navigator could record a positional fix. In those circumstances, if the boat went below sixty-eight feet, the periscope would be under the water, and anyone looking through the scope could not see. If depth was less than sixty-four feet, however, too much of the scope would be exposed, making it easier for any Soviet vessels in the area to discover us. For much of the time we were on station, the weather was rough. A "state three sea" on the surface made depth control a nightmare, and attempts to solve the problem required the constant use of the fairwater planes, which were noisier than the stern planes. That made the sonarmen's job more difficult, and all of that together tested the captain's patience. On several occasions, rough weather at periscope depth caused the boat to fluctuate between sixty and sixty-eight feet despite anything that could be—and everything that was—done by the diving officer or the planesmen. In those conditions, the captain barked at us, "Get me up! Six inches!" which was a virtual impossibility. More than once we came perilously close to breaching—a very undesirable situation when the nose goes down and the screw and the fantail section actually appear above the waterline. When that happens, the boat is completely compromised, and the only solution is to flood the auxiliary tanks and get the screw back under the water as soon as possible. The captain's reactions in these situations were not those of a man in control: Impatient and nervous, he did little to instill confidence in his crew.

We got better at depth control as the patrol wore on, but that was about the only excitement I can remember for those thirty days on station. Early on in the trip, Captain Shellman adopted a nonconfrontational approach to all contacts. If sonar reported a contact, especially one that might be a submarine, Shellman would often order a course change that would take us in the opposite direction. The crew began to refer to him as "old one-eighty out," because it seemed like he was unwilling to put us in a position where we could be discovered. This infuriated the spooks.

Spooks were additional riders sent by the National Security Agency to accompany submarines on patrol. Specially trained sailors, they were, essentially, spies sent to operate the very sophisticated electronic intelligence-gathering equipment in the ECM room. Because they were spies, we were ordered to keep our distance while they were on board: We were not to interact with them in any manner. They kept to themselves and so did we. From a security point of view, any interaction would potentially compromise them and us, as knowledge of their real identities could endanger their lives. Because their single purpose on board was to gather electronic information, it was well known in the submarine community that the spooks looked with disdain on those commanders who were not willing to take the necessary chances to let them do so. They referred to these cautious officers as "Charlie Tuna," or "Chicken of the Sea." We weren't on station long before the label was applied to Captain Shellman.

Then an incident involving the crew's love of popular music entered into the picture. A huge hubbub developed one day when someone inadvertently played the *Revolver* album by the Beatles on the entertainment system in the crew's mess. When the words to the song "Yellow Submarine" came out of the speakers, the news went through the boat like a virus, and people started singing it under their breath. COB Welsh said that his planesmen sang it one night while on watch, and XO DeMars put a stop to the practice almost immediately. ET2 John Buchanan recalled that "DeMars heard us singing it one day in the ECM space. He stuck his head in and said, 'If I hear it again you lose two stripes!' "

The singing stopped, and the song didn't play again for the remainder of the trip, but the damage was already done.

In hindsight, the underway criticism of Captain Shellman was unjustified. Frustrated, the crew believed that "if we have to be up here, we should be doing something!" Shellman had no prior spec op (special operations) experience, which, interestingly enough, was not uncommon among the submarine officer corps at the time. In truth, the only officer in the *Sturgeon* wardroom who did have spec op experience was XO DeMars. He made five patrols in the Pacific on board USS *Snook*, and in the course of his career, he would go on to make over ten, including the three that I made on board the *Sturgeon*.

A cautious man by nature, Shellman was commanding a brand new, very expensive boat with an inexperienced wardroom and crew. There were some patrol veterans on board, but almost all of the young guys had never been north before. Given that knowledge, a case can easily be made that a prudent approach to a first patrol—no matter how unpopular with the crew—was in everyone's best interest.

We remained in the operations area for a little more than a month before transit back to New London. It was common practice for the SUBLANT to award the Meritorious Unit Commendation Ribbon to submarines that completed successful patrols, and their captains would often be eligible for the Legion of Merit. On our return, however, Shellman received the Navy Commendation Medal—a less prestigious award—and the boat received nothing.

State Pier

We returned from patrol in November 1967 still assigned to submarine squadron ten, which meant that if there was no room at the submarine base, we tied up alongside USS *Fulton*, a submarine tender almost permanently attached to the State Pier in New London. As soon as we arrived in the tender's loving arms, the same crap about being squared away that had happened in Charleston took place again. Only this time, the tender made the mistake of upsetting Hank Marquette.

Born in Ashland, Wisconsin, Marquette shoveled coal in the fire room of a merchantman on Lake Superior at the age of fourteen. He joined the Navy in 1950 at the age of sixteen. As head of the auxiliary division on the *Sturgeon*, Marquette was a hard-drinking, no-nonsense chief machinist's mate, and he did not like to be messed with. One night he had been out on the town and had already had a few when the quarterdeck watch on board the *Fulton* stopped him as he came on board. He recalls the incident, saying, "I had a six-pack in a brown paper bag, and the bag busted, and they confiscated my beer."

Marquette got mad, and then he got even. The next time he had the duty, he waited until he was sure that the nightly movie was being shown in the mess hall on board the tender. He then blew the sanitary tank and vented over the side. The stench was horrible. Harassment from the tender ceased the next day, for the time being.

On a separate occasion, another member of the A gang, who to this day remains officially anonymous—although I suspect it was "Salt Water" Bell—packed the drain pump discharge with ice and then aligned the pumps with the sanitary tank. Usually the discharge hose would then be hooked up to a truck on the pier, and when the truck was full, the waste would be driven away. Only this time, the discharge hose was pointed toward the tender, and the pumps were turned on. The pressure built to the point at which a block of ice about six inches long was hurled toward the quarterdeck of the tender, followed by a dark brown stream of the most noxious liquid imaginable. The side of the tender was covered in excrement. Harassment from the tender once again ceased. One sure way to stop chickenshit in the Navy was a dose of the real thing.

As promised, when the *Sturgeon* returned from the northern run, YN1 Slack recommended me for the third class test, and the XO approved it. I took the examination and, like everyone else, waited on tenterhooks for the results, which came in increments. There were six sets of results. If you passed with flying colors, you made rate first increment and received the raise in pay immediately. Any of the subsequent increments led to the pay raise and change in grade months down the line, and your knowledge of your rate coincided with the increment you passed at. I made yeoman 3rd class on the sixth increment—by the skin of my teeth, as they say. Still, I had a profession that would allow me to stay on the boat.

I then began full-time work in the ship's office. Navy bureaucracy involved complicated sets of procedures and forms for everything. The new XO, Bruce DeMars, created an atmosphere on the boat that encouraged individual and crew achievement. So, when the next battery of examinations was announced in early 1968, he recommended me for the second class test. That caused a real controversy among the more senior members of the crew. You see, because I made rate sixth increment, I was scheduled to take the second class exam before I actually received the third class chevron. In the regular Navy, rate is difficult to come by. There is a great deal of competition, and it can often take years to move from one level to another. In the eyes of some of the chiefs, I appeared to be on an accelerated path paved by the XO's favoritism, and they were not happy about it. Most of them thought I would make second class before I made third class—an impossible scenario. For a while, I walked on eggshells through the boat. In any case, it didn't work out that way at all. I failed the second class test, and a month later I received my third class chevron. However, that test gave me a real leg up for the next time around, because it told me exactly what I needed to learn. DeMars knew what he was doing.

Part II

1968
Change of Command

Riding the Storm

O N JANUARY 22, 1968, the *Sturgeon* departed New London for a five-week ASW (antisubmarine warfare) operation in Georges Basin, the Gulf of Maine. USS *Seawolf* (SSN 575) acted as the target in an exercise designed to test our new fire control system for wire-guided torpedoes. The idea was for the *Seawolf* to make high-speed runs through the deep narrow canyon, which would pose a real test for our sonarmen. A serious echo existed in Georges Basin, but our sonar guys were up to the task. Finding *Seawolf* was not a problem—she was noisy, and we were not.

Sound travels much farther under the water, and the ocean is not a quiet place. STC Ted Lee, a very experienced chief, headed a sonar shack populated by guys like John Kuester, John Fitzsimmons, Jim Hartman, and Jim Jans. My favorite of the specialists on board the boat, sonarmen possess a unique physical gift: They have dog ears. They hear things that normal people cannot. If you went into the sonar shack and put on a set of earphones, you might hear something that sounded like the wash cycle of a Maytag top-loader. To our sonarmen, however, that would be a certain class of vessel, and depending on the sound signature, they could identify it by name. According to John Kuester, "We could do it by the fifth harmonic!"

On January 30, Lt. George Davis stood double duty in the control room as navigator and officer of the deck, while Captain Shellman lingered nearby. XO Bruce DeMars acted as fire control coordinator. The

Seawolf made her high-speed runs through the basin, and we tracked her. DeMars recalled, "I believe it was the third run. We had a very nice tracking solution, and I was about to recommend we shoot, when the solution rapidly fell apart. I thought he [the captain of the *Seawolf*] could not have turned south, as that was shallow water, so he must have turned north."

Davis recalled that Shellman was anxious to get the shot off because the *Seawolf* had eluded us twice before—including once by going to the surface. This time, the target was at the maximum range for the torpedo, and Davis was urging the captain to wait. Then sonar reported, "CON, sonar. Target has zigged to his left."

Davis and Shellman quickly referred to the charts and came to the conclusion that the *Seawolf* couldn't have done that because the water was too shallow. The boat would run into Georges Bank.

"Sonar, this is the captain," Shellman replied. "He couldn't have turned to his left." The sonarmen, however, were sure, "CON, Sonar. He turned to his left!"

DeMars remembered, "We tracked for several more minutes and then heard the most horrendous noise on the sonar. *Seawolf* had in fact turned south and run aground at about 20 knots."

Sonar immediately reported the grounding and, moments later, the emergency ballast tank blow that brought the *Seawolf* to the surface. Shellman then asked Davis just how accurate our charts were to determine whether we were out of position as well. Davis replied, "It's possible we could be as much as six miles off."

That did not sit well with the cautious Shellman. Sonar urged the captain to come to the surface to check on the *Seawolf*, but Kuester recalled that, "Shellman came up easy, took his time . . . [he] crept up."

DeMars remembered, "We went to periscope depth and tried to raise *Seawolf* on the UQC [an underwater telephone], but as we later surmised, it had been torn off. We finally established radio contact and stood by while rescue tugs arrived about a day later."

Machinist Mate 1st Class Al "Chauncey" Leach, who was on board *Seawolf* at the time, recalled the incident:

I was in the stern room, on watch in the after auxiliary machinery space when we hit. I was back there with Paul 'Ski' Chihockey, a first class quartermaster. We were fishing buddies, and he was back there winding the clocks. I was on port and starboard watches. I still remember it like it was yesterday. We hit on the bow, and we could feel the boat bounce, but we couldn't hear anything. I said 'That's a hell of a temperature change!'[1] When the stern hit, we still didn't hear anything, but we could feel the boat shake. Ski and I went to the upper level of the stern room, and all we could see was a yellow mist or fog. We had water spraying through the hull packings for the stern planes and the rudder. There were coffee tins piled around the rams for storage, and because of that, we couldn't get at the rams. At that point, we could feel that we were already starting up. Bob Hoke, a chief sonarman, was the chief of the watch. He initiated the emergency blow. We went up so fast—it was a hellacious up angle, and I slid on my ass right into the coffee cans. We had lost all the hydraulics. All the main and the vital hydraulic oil was on the floor in the stern room, and you could see the after bulkhead moving back and forth with the wave action topside. The rudder and the planes were hanging on by a thread. The whole turtleback section back there was just swinging.

A mess cook on board the *Seawolf* at the time, TM2 Richard Northrup remembered, "When we hit I was crawling through a small storage area under the mess hall. . . . I was as far forward from the hatch as I could get when the whole boat boomed, shook, and bounced nose up. I can remember hearing the watertight doors going 'bang, bang, bang' as they were being closed throughout the boat. Interestingly enough, there was never an alarm sounded throughout the whole incident. Somehow I got out of the compartment in time for the emergency blow, and we took the most audacious bow angle I can ever remember. It was huge! When I finally got a chance, I went back to the stern room and looked at the wooden bracing holding the aft bulkhead. Since our screws were bent and we had lost our forward sonar boom and a bit of the stern, we could not go any place, and we wallowed on the surface (not knowing whether she would stay afloat or not) for a day or so until a seagoing tug came and towed us in."

The commander of the submarine flotilla 2 would later issue citations "for outstanding performance and devotion to duty" to Leach, Chihockey, and ENC Fredrick T. Atwood for their actions in the engine room during the incident.

The submarine rescue vessel USS *Skylark* (ASR 20) arrived a day later and towed the disabled *Seawolf* back to New London. It took a week for them to get there, and on the way, her rudder fell completely off—all the way to the ocean floor. All this time, the *Sturgeon* stood by on the surface, and then the weather turned nasty.

Designed to travel submerged, attack submarines are not as fast or as responsive on the surface, and their cigar shape leaves them at the mercy of the ocean, so they can be tossed around like a cork. The *Sturgeon* suddenly found herself, as the storm approached, unable to submerge. Normally we would just go down, get as deep as possible, and ride it out in relative comfort. Not this time. We could not lower the radar mast—it simply would not go down. Located in the trunk of the sail, the motor for the mast was notorious for breaking down. We raised the radar mast only when the boat was on the surface, and the seal tested at no deeper than sixty feet. So, just like the mast, we were stuck, and ended up being forced to ride out the storm on the surface for a full three days.

At first, it wasn't too bad. Some guys got sick right away, but others who had better "sea legs" lasted longer. Eventually, however, the entire crew became seasick. The only solution was to go to bed and hope that when you laid down, you would feel a little better. Most of the crew walked around the boat with a bucket or a can of some sort around their necks, which made the concept of eating anything impossible. After a day of no food, however, you do get hungry. That's when things became surreal.

The crew's mess posted two documents in plain sight, the plan of the day, signed by the XO, and the weekly menu, signed by the captain. The plan of the day was the yeoman's responsibility and could be altered if necessary. Because the cooks were part of the supply division, the menu fell under the jurisdiction of the store-keeper, who typed it up and gave it to the cooks. They, in turn, sub-mitted it to the captain for approval. Once signed by the captain, the menu was etched in stone, and not even Congress could make any changes to it.

So, at the height of the storm, the scheduled meals included hot dogs with beans & sauerkraut for dinner, followed by Joe Bright's chili for lunch the next day. Men about to assume the watch would emerge from the bow compartment, walk toward the crew's mess, get one whiff of the sauerkraut, and then turn around and scramble back to the enlisted head. It was misery.

The storm also affected watches in the control room. On the sur-face, the planesman and helmsman responsibilities changed a bit. The stern planesman became a lookout on the bridge.

Cut into the sail just behind the bridge, where the officer of the deck or the captain stood, was another, smaller slot known as the lookout "Pookah," which accommodated one man. With the aid of binoculars, the lookout's single responsibility was to identify surface contacts of any kind. We rotated these watches on an hourly basis. Prepped with foul-weather gear and wearing a "Mae West" (lifejacket), I made the ascent to the bridge at the appropriate time to relieve my buddy Dick Austin as the lookout. Austin took one look at me and said, "Am I glad to see you! It's all yours!"

And with that, he descended to the safety of the control room.

Lt. John Naeve Pechauer was the officer of the deck, and he instructed me to chain myself to the superstructure as a precaution. A quick observation showed enormous wave height and extremely strong winds. I doubled that chain. With visibility impaired, the boat rolled significantly to port and back to starboard. My attempts to look through the binoculars proved hopeless. If either of us fell overboard, there would be no chance of recovery.

Not more than fifteen minutes later, things started to get really bad. At one point, my left arm hung over the side of the sail as I held on to the binoculars with the other. The boat rolled significantly to port, and when I turned that direction, the water rose up over my arm and the horizon was at eye level. We then rolled to starboard and took a steep pitch down. When the boat rolled back to port, the water broke over my head. That went on for while. The wind became so strong that I found myself unable to breathe normally. I had to turn to the leeward side to exhale. We experienced 30-degree rolls and larger pitch angles. Horizontal rain also ensued, and everything turned white and cold.

All this time, the captain attempted to find a course that would allow us the best chance to ride the storm out. Every time he altered course, however, something else would happen. Either the pitch would increase, or the rolls would get more dramatic. It was a roller-coaster ride and, by now, officially dangerous. I was more than a little scared. Pechauer, however, was rumored to be an ex-destroyer sailor, and he was in his element, determined to bend Mother Nature to his will. Then we heard the voice of the captain, "Bridge, this is the captain. I think we should bring the watch into the control room. It's now about a state ten sea. I think we should bring it down before someone goes over the side."

According to Ron Jones of the National Weather Service, a state ten sea on the Beaufort wind scale includes "wind speeds of 88–102 MPH, 30 foot seas, and very high waves. The sea surface is white and there is considerable tumbling." It's the equivalent of a category 2 hurricane. Pechauer, however, remained undaunted, "Captain, I think the boat's doing really well after the last course change, and I think we can . . ."

I didn't wait to hear the rest. I unchained myself, crawled over to the hatch, opened it, and headed down. Pechauer looked at me and asked, "Where are you going?"

I answered, "Lieutenant, the captain said 'bring the watch into Control,' and that's where I'm going!"

When I landed in the control room, I told diving officer Hank Marquette what happened. I thought surely I'd land on report for leaving my post, but Marquette just laughed: "Go below and dry off. Warm up, get a cup of coffee and then get back here!"

Nothing was ever said. That was the only incident in my time on board the *Sturgeon* when I actually feared for my life. That storm took its toll on the boat, as well. It tore the cover of the ship's horn completely off, and the radar mast, of course, needed attention. That exercise in the Gulf of Maine had other consequences, too, but we wouldn't realize them until many years later. With the *Seawolf* incapacitated and under repair in the shipyard for at least a year, she could not keep to her scheduled departure to the Mediterranean later that spring, so SUB-LANT scrambled another boat to keep that commitment. The boat they chose to send, USS *Scorpion* (SSN 589), never came back.

"83"

Our arrival at Electric Boat on March 3, 1968, for postshakedown availability (PSA) marked the *Sturgeon*'s last trip under the command of Captain Shellman. A new captain reported on board, and the change of command ceremony was scheduled for March 22 on the sub base. With PSA anticipated to last for over two months, work on the boat would happen on an around-the-clock basis, which meant there would be no opportunity to sleep on board. The bunks in the bow compartment were removed to facilitate the installation of a new sonar dome, and the crew were transferred to an ancient and musty barge for living quarters. Only a few men decided to stay there. The rest of us headed off to find suitable accommodations "on the beach."

One well-known, well-worn house just up the hill from the Electric Boat main gate—44 Poquonnock Road—ended up housing a bunch of us, including Dick Austin and myself in one room. The house belonged to Marian Reed, who also owned the infamous Elfie's, the bar where we paid our weekly rent. A local legend, Marian owned real estate all over Groton, Connecticut, including the aforementioned Elfie's and the Port-hole Café in Groton Long Point. A long-standing rumor said that she was Jack Nelson's lover. Others said they were just friends. Nobody ever confirmed it, but on the boat, it was generally accepted to be true. However, nobody ever mentioned it to Nelson. Nelson worked for Marian when the boat was in port, and after he retired from the Navy, he tended bar at the Porthole Café for years. The two remain friends to this day.

We stayed in that house on Poquonnock Road until the day Bill Drake announced to Austin, Denny Schulz, and me, "I've got us an apartment! Joey Chitwood moved out, so the place is now mine."

Chitwood was a "Boomer" sailor on the USS *George Washington* who, up until then, shared this apartment with Drake.

"Where?" we asked.

Drake replied, "The third floor of a house at 83 George Avenue, not far from here. We can walk to it. It's owned by this old Russian couple. The place has three bedrooms, a living room and a kitchen. It's perfect. Sixty bucks a month, and we pay the electric bill."

With that, the "Snake Ranch" known as 83 came into being. Over the course of the next three years, Bill Drake, Denny Schulz, Dick Austin, Barry Avery, Thom Keaney, Harry Dunn, Roger Windon, Max Wolf, and I all took up residence there at one time or another.

At the top of a steep stairway leading to the third floor, 83 featured five small rooms, with the bathroom, marked by the sign "Enlisted Head" above the door frame, located across the landing from the entrance to the apartment. The only heat came from an ancient oil stove in the kitchen and from the electric space heaters we found it necessary to purchase. The house's very poor—if any—insulation made the winter a real challenge. On more than one occasion, someone walked into the bathroom to discover the water in the toilet bowl frozen. If we turned on more than one space heater at a time, we would blow a fuse. So early on, Drake jury-rigged a solution by placing pennies behind the fuses in the basement. At that point, the electric bill began to rival the usually astronomical phone bill, and it's a small wonder that the place never exploded into flames.

Drake

From Corning, New York, machinist's mate William Arthur Drake enlisted in the Navy before he graduated from high school because, as he said, "They were after me!"

Raised on a farm and with no plans to attend college, Drake was a prime candidate to be drafted. He chose to be proactive about his military service instead, and the Navy allowed him to enlist on the 120-day deferred program before he graduated from high school. Four months later, in the coldest part of the year, Drake found himself at Great Lakes, Illinois, standing dumpster watches on the Grinder. The Grinder was a parade ground surrounded by dumpsters. Watches were assigned to ensure no one stole them—as if anyone would. Dumpster duty in cold weather was misery.

When he enlisted, Drake was promised an A school on graduation, but that didn't happen. A lot of that sort of thing went on back then. On the day Drake was to state his "three wishes," he mentioned aviation machinist's mate as one option. The interviewer ignored him and then asked, "What do you think about submarines?" Drake replied, "They're OK, I guess." The book slammed shut, and that was it. Drake had officially volunteered for submarines. A few weeks later, he found himself at submarine school in Groton, where, as he recalls, "A grinder was a sandwich, and pop was called soda!"

After graduation from submarine school, Drake reported directly to an unfinished USS *Sturgeon* in the shipyard, and when Dennis Schulz made 3rd class fire control technician, the COB made Drake leading seaman. Drake passed his qualification test while underway in the fall of 1967, and with no extra sets of dolphins on board, COB Welsh gave him his personal set. Drake has them to this day.

Schulz

In 1965, Dennis Michael Schulz, of Euclid, Ohio, discovered himself on college academic probation. Realizing the potential consequences of his name not appearing on the college roll, he enlisted in November of that year.

"The draft was going, and if I wasn't going to go to college, I was going to enlist. I chose the Navy because I had a cousin who was in the Navy, and as soon as I enlisted, the Navy lied to me for the first time. I was supposed to go to boot camp in San Diego, but when I got on the train, they told me, 'Oh, there's meningitis in San Diego, so we're sending you to Great Lakes instead!' Yeah . . . right!"

Because Schulz had enough college experience, he was an instant seaman, and at the top of his "three wishes" list appeared aviation aerographer's mate. Aerographer's mates are the Navy's meteorological and oceanographic experts. They learn to use instruments that monitor weather characteristics such as air pressure, temperature, humidity, and wind speed and direction, and they then distribute these data to aircraft, ships, and shore. To Schulz, it sounded interesting. The Navy had other ideas. The interviewer told him, "No. What you really want to do is fly helicopters!"

Schulz was incredulous. "So, they sat me down in a dark room with three people at the table and questioned me in great detail. It really scared me, freaked me out a bit, and I guess I didn't do so well. Thankfully, my career as a helicopter pilot went away. After that, I volunteered for submarines because I had a cousin who was on the *Nautilus*."

A train took him to submarine school in Groton, and on completion, he reported on board the *Sturgeon* on Good Friday, April 8, 1966. With the boat still in the shipyard and uninhabitable, he stayed in "some flophouse on Bridge Street for the weekend, and then I moved into a house across the street from the north gate of Electric Boat with Ron

Gochmonsky. Later on, I shared a place with Hank Horry and Fred Davies. After that, I moved to 83."

COB Welsh made Schulz the leading seaman and eventually steered him toward fire control technician as a rate. Schultz made 3rd class on his second attempt.

Austin

Richard Kenneth Austin originally hailed from Spokane, Washington, but his family moved around a lot because of his father's business. Austin attended high school in Oregon, and in 1966, he traveled to Alaska.

"I enlisted in February of 1966 in Anchorage," he remembered, "because that's the only place I could get into the Navy. They were full up everywhere else."

The youngest of the four of us, Austin went to boot camp and store-keeper A school in San Diego and then to submarine school in New London. He reported on board the *Sturgeon* in late 1966, with the boat still in the shipyard, and spent his first months on board as a mess cook before being transferred to the seaman gang.

In the summer of 1967, SK1 Lin "Mac" McCollum, the boat's resident "cumshaw" king, decided to leave the Navy, and Austin took his place. McCollum had achieved near legendary status for his ability to acquire goods and services in exchange for a large can of coffee, often to the chagrin of Cook Jack Nelson, but then again, "Nellie" couldn't argue too much with the man who got him the coffee in the first place. Austin, I, and others who later engaged in the art of cumshaw all learned from a real master.

Life "On the Beach"

The phone bill at 83 always topped the rent, usually being more than twice as much, because both Drake and Schulz were conducting long-distance love affairs. Drake met Caroline Van Woert at a postgraduation party. Although they attended the same high school, they never really knew each other before then. Schulz met Pat Faiken while at home on leave from boot camp before he left for submarine school: "One day I went back to my high school to pick up my sister, and Pat jumped into the front seat next to me. That was it!"

Drake married Caroline in August 1968. We all went to the wedding in Corning, New York, and just a month later we were at sea on a long run. Schulz married Pat in 1970 after he got out of the Navy. Both couples are still together.

After the wedding, Bill and Caroline moved into 83 until they could find an apartment of their own. Once, when Bill had weekend duty, Austin, Schulz, and I kidnapped Caroline and took her to some club at Misquamicut Beach outside of Westerly, Rhode Island. Caroline wasn't old enough to drink, but they weren't too strict about checking identification there. In fact, when we first moved into the apartment, only Schulz was old enough to legally drink, and we had to send him out for the beer. Caroline kept telling us that we were trying to corrupt her. She was right.

"You guys got me snockered!" she recalled.

It only took a couple of drinks, but she made breakfast for us in the morning.

There was always music at 83. Schulz owned a really good stereo system that he kept in a closet in the living room. Musical tastes within the house varied. Schulz loved Simon and Garfunkel and Wes Montgomery. I was entranced by the Beatles, Janis Joplin, Bob Dylan, and Cream, and Sam Bass introduced me to Miles Davis and Dave Brubeck. Everyone loved the Motown groups like the Supremes, the Four Tops, and the Temptations. The only real dissent came from Drake, who never had any use for Dylan, saying, "The man just can't sing!"

No one knows for sure who started the practice of answering the phone "83!" although I suspect Schulz. It stuck, however, and no matter who was there, or what was going on, that's how everyone answered the phone. The apartment quickly became party central—and the parties were epic.

Submariners work hard and play hard. My time on board *Sturgeon* was a little more than a thousand days. During that period, disregarding the three months in the shipyard for PSA, we were at sea approximately 78 percent of the time—90 percent of that submerged—often doing dangerous things, and when we returned to port, we needed to blow off steam. The submariner's principal off-duty occupations included the consumption of alcohol and the pursuit of women, not necessarily in that order, and our crew was no exception. While in port, the four of us, always assisted by a few shipmates, consumed a healthy amount of beer, and when we gave parties, the amount we drank was staggering.

One Monday morning, after a weekend off that did not feature a party, Drake and I carried out about a dozen or so empty cases of beer to the trash. When the garbage man saw us, he commented that it "must have been a good party!" Drake responded, "There was no party."

The guy wouldn't believe him, so, Drake took his telephone number and promised to invite him the next time we did have a party. When that garbage man showed up and witnessed our crew in operation, he was astonished.

We invited everybody to our parties, almost everybody came, and they all brought booze with them. The kitchen table would be awash in bottles of wine, gin, rye, whisky, vodka, rum, tequila, brandy, peppermint schnapps, and mixers of all kinds. The refrigerator would be full of beer, and on several occasions, we filled the bathtub with beer covered in ice.

Caroline remembered the morning after one particular party: "I woke up, and Schulz was curled up asleep on the kitchen table, surrounded by bottles."

The parties at 83 did not always end the evening: Sometimes they acted as a prelude to a night on the town. A lot has been said about college fraternity parties, and there have even been highly successful movies on the subject. In truth, frat boys pale next to submarine sailors. No frat boy ever had to drive a nuclear-powered submarine the next day, and no frat boy ever went on a "turkey shoot" at the Dolphin with Hank Horry.

Ken Schack remembered his first day on board *Sturgeon*, "I ran into a gentleman named Hank Horry." Horry said, "You're new!" To which Schack replied, "Yep." Horry declared, "Turkey shoot tonight, the Dolphin 7:00 PM!"

"I got there about fifteen minutes late," Schack remembered. "Hank said, 'You're late. Catch up.'" Schack reminisced, "Hank was on the left and Rog Windon was on the right. Between was my stool, and there were five shots and five glasses of beer in front of me."

Hank Horry was a 1st class quartermaster who stood six feet three inches; Rog Windon was a 2nd class fire control technician who stood six feet four, and Schack himself stood close to six feet four. These were the biggest guys on the boat, and they could hold their liquor. A turkey shoot was an evening of Austin Nichol's 101 proof Wild Turkey bourbon with beer chasers, and it was not for the faint of heart. That was how Horry and Windon welcomed Schack to the *Sturgeon*—a boat whose alcohol consumption was the stuff of legend.

On Bank Street in downtown New London existed three submarine bars, the Submarine Restaurant, Ernie's, and the Dolphin Cafe. Never to be confused with café society, these joints featured such delicacies as pickled eggs, beef jerky, peanuts, popcorn, and potato chips. These were the places that submariners went to get drunk. Every boat had a preference among these three, and the Dolphin, run by two guys named Sock and Bob, was *Sturgeon*'s bar of choice, actually one of two. The other was an Italian family restaurant and bar on Poquonnock Road in Groton called Gino's, which sat one block away from 83 at the bottom of a very short hill. At Gino's, we watched football games over beer and meatball sandwiches or had a few before we went dancing. When *Sturgeon* returned from a patrol, however, the Dolphin was the place you ended up your first night back, where you shed over sixty days of underwater confinement, where all of your inhibitions disappeared and you were set free to howl at the moon or sing as loud as you could to jukebox hits like "Sky Pilot" by the Animals until 1:00 AM. It's where you "drank your Dolphins," danced on the tables, danced on the bar, and never got in trouble with the proprietors for any of that or a whole lot more.

After the Dolphin closed, we crossed the bridge for breakfast at a diner on Route 12 before heading home around two in the morning. On some occasions, however, the night didn't end there. Schulz was a lot of fun when he'd had a few—and with him, it only took a few. The owner of the house diagonally across from 83 had a flagstaff in his front yard, and he never took the flag down. More than once Schulz and I held colors on the lawn at 0200. With great solemnity, we lowered the flag, folded it according to regulation, and placed it in the mailbox, all the while humming "Taps." We then went to our apartment to sleep. In the morning, we'd get up and put on our uniforms, and as we left the house, we'd see our neighbor raising his flag. I'm sure he knew we did it, but he never said a word. We'd then pile into Austin's red VW hatchback and ride down River Road to our jobs on board a brand new submarine. It was all very innocent, and in retrospect, joyous.

The Water Tower Incident

One night, toward the end of the PSA at Electric Boat, Drake, Cornibert, Schulz, Austin, and I were at 83 having a few beers. Suddenly, Drake stood up and said, "Let's paint the water tower."

The water tower at Electric Boat was one of several landmarks used as navigational markers to keep the boat in the center of the channel as it traversed the Thames River to and from the submarine base. In the control room during the maneuvering watch, you could hear the navigator, as he looked through the number 2 periscope, call the markers out to the quartermaster for the "fix": "Mark the bearing number 2! . . . The EB water tower . . . Mark! . . . The state pier water tower . . . Mark!

. . . The center of the bridge . . . Mark! . . . The Groton monument . . . Mark!"

Drake's idea was to climb up to the walkway that surrounded the Electric Boat water tower and paint our boat's numbers large enough that they would be seen by anyone who would come up the river. This required very little thought. It was dark outside and after 2100. No one would see us.

"Where are we going to get the paint and the brushes?" I asked. Drake replied, "From the Paint Shop at EB." I said, "You mean we're just going to walk into the Paint Shop and ask for them?" His reply was, "Why not?" I wasn't so sure: "Do you think they'll give'm to us?" But Drake knew better: "Sure . . . it's been done before." I said "OK . . . let's go!"

Austin, convinced that we were all going to get arrested, wanted no part of it, and he stayed behind at the apartment. So, fueled by alcohol, Drake, Cornibert, Schulz, and I headed down to the paint shop at Electric Boat. We walked in, and the guy in the shop looked at us and said, "What can I do for you?" Drake told him that we needed a gallon of paint and four brushes and promised, "We'll bring back what we don't use." The guy asked, "What are you going to do with it?" and Drake told him, "Paint the boat's number on the water tower." The guy said, "OK!" handed us a gallon of paint and four brushes, and off we went.

"We'll bring back what we don't use!!! That was cute." Cornibert teased Drake. "Shut up!" he said, "We got the paint, didn't we?" I asked him, "What if somebody stops us?" His answer was, "They won't. Just keep walking."

Men on a mission, we headed directly to the target. Now, the old water tower at Electric Boat was pretty big. The shipyard was built on a steep hill, and the tower was visible from almost anywhere in that part of Groton. It had to be a hundred feet up to the walkway. With a casual disregard for the almost absurd level of danger involved in this enterprise, we scrambled up the access ladder to the walkway and began the task. Drake acted the daredevil and stood on the railing, with absolutely nothing between him and the ground below, while he painted "637" in very large strokes. Cornibert and I filled in the gaps. Schulz, however, showed signs of acrophobia and was moving slowly. He had made it only halfway up the ladder when the roving security guard spotted him. If that hadn't happened, we just might have gotten away with it. The guard yelled at us, "All right, come on down from there immediately!" We ignored him. "You are under arrest for trespassing and the defacing of private property. Come down immediately." Obviously, he'd been through this before.

Drake called down to him, "We'll be down when we're finished!" And that's what we did. We completed the task and descended to be arrested, along with Schulz. The guard escorted us back to the boat and handed us over to the duty officer, Lt. Dennis Moritz. Moritz was not happy with us. He read us the riot act and confined us to quarters until morning. Because all of the bunks on the boat had been removed to facilitate the PSA, the official crew's quarters was on an ancient, dingy barge two piers away and out of sight. "So, we're confined to the barge, Sir?" we asked. "That's right," was the response. "Yes, Sir!"

We saluted and quickly walked away. There was no watch posted on the barge, so we went back to the apartment and finished the beer. The next morning, we were all a little nervous—until the new captain arrived and heard about our exploits. He took one look at our artwork through the periscope and just smiled. Nothing else was ever said about it. The boat's number remained visible for months.

"Bo"

William Louis "Bo" Bohannan of Willcox, Arizona, graduated from the University of New Mexico in 1953 with a degree in architectural engineering. He served on board USS *Walker* (DDE 517) as antisubmarine warfare and gunnery officer and then graduated from submarine school in 1957. He qualified in submarines on board USS *Grenadier* (SS 525), where he served as supply officer, engineer, operations officer, and navigator. In 1959, he transferred to the USS *Robert E. Lee* (SSBN 601)(BLUE), where he qualified for command while serving as weapons officer. That time was followed by stints at submarine forces in the Atlantic fleet, nuclear power school, prototype training, and the Polaris command course. He served as XO on board USS *Francis Scott Key* (SSBN 657) and then reported to naval reactors for instruction. Following prospective commanding officer school at New London, Connecticut, he reported on board *Sturgeon* in February 1968.

The official change of command ceremony took place March 22, 1968, on the submarine base. All of us who were there that day noticed immediately that, from a physical standpoint, Captain Bohannan was everything that Captain Shellman was not. He was tall and athletic in his manner, and as he reviewed the crew, he smiled. He seemed excited about taking command, and he made an overt gesture of speaking directly to the COB, which did not go unnoticed.

However, the boat was in the shipyard, and it would be weeks before Bohannan would take her to sea. That first short trip allowed him to run some drills, test the new sonar equipment, and see what he had for a crew. We were scheduled to return on Friday, May 31. On the way in, we hit fog at Race Rock, and the navigator suggested to the officer of the deck that he order all stop and have the radiomen call into the submarine base for the tugs. There was a long-standing practice on the boat, instituted by Captain Shellman, that if visibility was bad, the tugs would be sent for, and they would push us up the river to the base like a wounded animal. Because we had to wait for the tugs to scramble from the base and travel all the way down the river to meet us, hours were added to the maneuvering watch, and everyone on the boat developed a case of so-called channel fever. It had happened repeatedly all through 1967, and it did nothing to endear Captain Shellman to the crew.

I was the helmsman at the time when the order for all stop was given. It was mere moments later that Captain Bohannan appeared right next to me and asked, "Why are we at all stop?" I replied, "The officer of the deck ordered all stop, Sir." Navigator George Davis chimed in, "Captain, the fog is pretty thick, and . . . " Bohannan didn't even wait for him to finish. He was gone, up the ladder in the trunk to the bridge. IC3 Barry Avery recalled, "My maneuvering watch was the phone talker in the conning tower. I'll tell you . . . we couldn't see a thing. Bohannan came up and said, 'Don't you know how to navigate with radar? Let's get going.'"

Moments later, in control, we heard, "All ahead two thirds!" I answered, "All ahead two thirds, Aye! Answers all ahead two thirds!" The response came, "Maneuvering, make speed for ten knots!" And the response was, "Make speed for ten knots, Aye!" The captain came below a moment later and said to Davis, "Blow the ship's horn if you have to. That's what it's there for."

Bohannan then checked with ET2 John Buchanan, who manned the radar. Buchanan recalled that, the captain came in and asked, "What does the radar show?" Buchanan's response was, "Well, Captain, there's the lighthouse, the bridge, the state pier, EB, and there's the pier we usually tie up to." The captain replied, "OK, we're goin' in!" and then he went back to his cabin.

Bohannan not only brought us in on time but did it without the aid of the tugs. In fact, when the tugs showed up to assist, he waved them off and tied up to pier ten south at the submarine base unassisted, with only six bell commands to the helmsman, seemingly to prove it could be done. The effect on the crew was startling. An electrical jolt, it told everyone that things were going to be very different from that point on—and they were. There was a sea change in onboard attitude.

Other than for operational purposes, Captain Shellman had seldom engaged in any personal communication with his crew. Except for those moments when I answered direct commands as the helmsman, I never spoke with the man. Captain Bohannan was the opposite. He seemed to know that, as captain, he could only be as good as his crew, and he wanted every man on board, regardless of rank or seniority, truly invested in the importance of his particular task. He spoke to enlisted men and officers alike, and he showed a genuine concern for all of us. If he was sitting in his stateroom and you walked by, or if you went by him in a passageway, he would startle you by asking, "How are you doing?" That never happened under Shellman. Bohannan made us all *want* to follow him.

Bruce Kuykendall said, "When he came on board . . . that's when I first knew he would be a good CO. Every night he'd come down and grab me. He'd say, 'Are you going home yet?' 'No.' 'When are you going home?' 'Obviously when you're done with me.' 'OK, I want to go through the air system . . . valve by valve.' 'OK.' Two days later, 'I want to go through the trim system, valve by valve.' I took that man from the bow to the stern, twice, sometimes three times a week. Of all the captains I served with, he was the slickest one in the world."

In addition, Bohannan was a graduate of the University of New Mexico—an outsider—different from the Annapolis so-called "ring knockers," and because of that, the crew liked him even more. Everyone was anxious to find out what he would be like in a real situation. We didn't have long to wait.

Underway in an Hour

The storekeeper and the yeoman did not stand duty in port, but on arrival we were required to open the incoming mail and deal with anything that needed immediate attention before we could go on liberty. Usually we were the last to leave. On Saturday morning, the day after we arrived back from that first short trip with Captain Bohannan, Austin and I returned to the boat to check the mail again. We finished our duties by early afternoon, hopped into his red Volkswagen hatchback, and scooted down River Road to George Avenue. We walked into our apartment, opened a beer, and then the phone rang. Austin answered it: "83!"

"Who is it?" I asked. "It's the Duty Officer . . . says we have to be back on the boat. We're getting underway in an hour!" I answered, "Bullshit!"

Nothing in the U.S. Navy gets underway in an hour unless it is really serious, and to scramble a nuclear submarine from the submarine base in that time frame would take something like an act of war. Then Austin heard something else. "OK, that was the captain. He said get back to the boat, now!"

We hustled back to the boat and were told to sit tight. Orders would be forthcoming. Hours went by before we were told to "relax, but don't leave the boat." We spent a restless night on board, and at quarters the next morning there was still no explanation, but we were instructed to make a phone call to notify our families that we would be leaving again. I went up to the phone booth at the head of the pier and called my parents. I told them that I didn't know what was happening but to watch the news.

Before noon on Sunday, the captain backed the boat away from the pier unassisted and headed down the river, ignoring the wake restrictions. When we hit water deep enough, somewhere near Point Alpha, we submerged, and as soon as Marquette reported that he had "trimmed the boat," the captain ordered "All ahead flank!" And we headed across the Atlantic Ocean, with the throttle wide open, on what was the saddest trip any of us ever made. The *Scorpion* (SSN 589) was overdue and was presumed lost somewhere near the Azores. We were part of a group of submarines and surface ships sent to the last position she was heard from.

We departed from New London so hastily that the navigator discovered he was somewhat unprepared. Davis reported to the captain that he was without the proper LORAN charts for that part of the ocean. Short for long-range navigation, the LORAN system used a series of low-frequency radio transmissions from several different stations to determine the position of the boat. Without the charts, it would be really difficult to get an accurate fix. Despite the incredibly serious nature of the mission, Bohannan found a moment to show the great sense of wit we all came to know. He replied, "Well, break out the sextant!"

Captain Bohannan later told me that Davis' face had a look that said, "Where do we store the sextant, and can I remember how to use it?" For the record, Davis was a good navigator, and he knew how to use a sextant, but the captain startled him with the suggestion that he might have to.

We steamed across the Atlantic at top speed. Engineering Chief of the Watch Homer Ross reported that it was 140°F in the engine room. We arrived in an area south of the Azores and spent about ten days actively pinging with the sonar. Sonarman John Fitzsimmons recalled, "We were searching for underwater mountains that *Scorpion* might have run into."

The whole exercise was an act of desperation. By that time, we all knew *Scorpion* was lost. Eventually, the captain contacted the senior officer present afloat and asked to be released because we were short on food. We had left the base in such a hurry that we hadn't had the opportunity to reload provisions for any kind of lengthy deployment. We returned to New London with heavy hearts. Ninety-nine men lost their lives on *Scorpion*. It remains the last submarine in the U.S. Navy to be lost at sea.

Not everyone on the boat made that trip. Machinist's Mate Dennis Roger Cloutier reported on board the afternoon of May 31 and was given weekend liberty, so he returned to his family's home in Hartford. Cloutier and his family were just about to go to Catholic Mass Sunday morning when he received the call, and his parents drove him to Groton. They arrived in time to see the boat going down the river to sea. Dennis reported to the squadron, and they immediately radioed an offer to send him out on a tug. The captain declined because Cloutier was brand new, not qualified to stand any watches, and wouldn't have been of any use at that point.

Gary Louis Cornibert, from Commack, New York, had hitchhiked to Long Island to see his fiancée, Lois Palmeri of Central Islip. They had met at Suffolk Community College before Gary joined the Navy and were to be married later in the summer. Cornibert arrived home to discover that he had to turn around and head right back. His mother drove him part of the way, across the Throgs Neck Bridge, and he hitched the rest. He was walking down River Road toward the submarine base when he saw *Sturgeon* headed down the river. Years later, he told me, "My heart just sank. Watching the boat leave without me was the loneliest feeling I have ever had."

The trip affected civilian lives as well. On June 8 in Stamford, Connecticut, our old shipmate Thomas O'Neal married Elizabeth Ann "Betty" Stock of Cresson, Pennsylvania. Tommy was a reactor operator on the shakedown cruise and then got out of the Navy. Although many submariners had been invited from several different boats, none attended Tom and Betty's reception: All of his old friends were at sea.

The search for *Scorpion* continued for five months before the wreckage was found in eleven thousand feet of water four hundred miles southwest of the Azores. At the time, speculation as to what caused the boat to sink was rife. The theories ran the gamut from the sublime to the ridiculous. Some tabloid newspapers, and even *Reader's Digest*, suggested that a Soviet death ray was responsible. It would be years before the Freedom of Information Act lifted the veil of secrecy and revealed the results of the official inquest. To this day, it is still speculative in nature, and the true reason for the boat's demise may never be known. However, Stephen Johnson's fine book *Silent Steel* examines the incident in depth and provides a detailed look at the events that led up to the tragedy.

Poseidon's Kingdom

On the transit back to New London, we received instructions to pass through a specific quadrant in the ocean for one hour on the surface. As we came shallow, I realized it was my turn in the watch rotation, and once again, I would be standing lookout with Lt. Dennis Moritz as the officer of the deck. After being submerged for long periods of time, any opportunity to go topside while underway was a real treat, but based on my last experience on the bridge, back in early February, I wasn't exactly looking forward to it. The klaxon sounded three times, and Fred Davies announced on the public address system, "Surface, surface, surface!" As soon as we were up, I cracked the hatch and headed up the ladder in the trunk to the bridge. This time almost everything was different. Once again, it was late in the afternoon, and the sun was about to disappear at the end of what could only be called a gray day. The sky was still light, with dark cumulus clouds in the distance, but the ocean was in a state that I had never witnessed before. It was almost dead calm, with no whitecaps visible for as far as the eye could see, which was unusual. Instead, we were moving through extremely long, deep swells that appeared to be part of an enormous, undulating, shiny blue-black piece of satin that extended in every direction all the way to the horizon. Although it was very peaceful and profoundly beautiful, I was overcome with a great sense of foreboding. It was as if Poseidon himself was whispering, "You see, I can be this way as well, or I can turn on you in a moment. You'll never really know." It was, in the end, more menacing than the state ten conditions in the Gulf of Maine. I remained topside for the entire hour before we dove again. Before and since, I have never experienced a moment when I felt a greater respect for the immeasurable power of the sea.

Eight Seconds

When we returned to the submarine base, we spent the rest of that summer preparing for another deployment in the fall. One of the direct results of the *Scorpion* incident was an increased emphasis on safety procedures. The submarine base had a trainer set up to drill responses to specific catastrophe scenarios. A simulator, much like those used by the airlines to train their pilots, was set up as a diving station for a nuclear-powered submarine, and all boats were scheduled for retraining.

Thus, all three watch sections of our boat made their way up to the trainer. Austin and I stood watches together for over two years, and not just regular planesmen/helmsmen watches, but also the maneuvering watch and battle stations pairings. Gruff, no-nonsense Hank Marquette was our chief of the watch in most of those situations. Marquette was secretly a lot of fun, once you got to know him, and a great diving officer. We spent days running a series of drills—fire, flooding, collision—every scenario for every compartment on the boat, all at different speeds and different depths. At the sound of each alarm, we attempted to accomplish everything possible to achieve positive buoyancy in the shortest period of time. We failed test after test. Finally, we beat the simulator. We discovered that, in the worst situation imaginable, we had eight seconds to do everything necessary to get the boat to the surface, and even then, you could never really be sure it would work.

At twenty-one years old, my life depended on an eight-second survival plan. When your everyday actions are based on that knowledge, even for only a short period of time, it affects the way you make decisions for the rest of your life.

Back Home

The news that greeted us on our return wasn't the best we'd ever heard. In truth, the storm we experienced in the Gulf of Maine seemed to be indicative of the way the year would go.

In January, North Korea seized the U.S. Navy intelligence ship USS *Pueblo* (AGER 2), charging it had entered into the communist nation's territorial waters on a spying mission. One man was killed in the attack. The captain, Cdr. Lloyd Bucher, and his crew were kept as prisoners under terrible conditions for almost a year. In South Vietnam, Viet Cong and North Vietnamese soldiers attacked both strategic and civilian locations in what became known as the Tet Offensive. The Viet Cong seized part of the U.S. embassy in Saigon for six hours before it was retaken, and the communist troops who took control of the ancient capital of

Hue killed an estimated six thousand civilians before they again lost control of the city.

In February, the United States fell in love with Peggy Fleming when she won the gold medal in women's figure skating at the Winter Olympic Games in Grenoble, France.

In early March, Gen. William Westmoreland asked for 206,000 more troops in Vietnam. Two weeks later, he was relieved of his duties in the wake of the Tet disaster. Troop strength under Westmoreland reached over half a million and still he wanted more. Gen. Creighton Abrams succeeded him.

On March 31, President Johnson appeared on national television and announced, "I shall not seek, and I will not accept, the nomination of my party for another term as your president." CBS News anchorman Walter Cronkite's nightly commentary on the progress of the Vietnam War led to Johnson's decision. Cronkite, who had been at Hue in January, said: "Who won and who lost in the great Tet Offensive against the cities? I'm not sure. It is increasingly clear to this reporter that the only rational way out will be to negotiate, not as victors but as an honorable people who lived up to their pledge to defend democracy, and did the best they could." Johnson called the commentary a "turning point," and stated that if he had "lost Cronkite, he'd lost Mr. Average Citizen."

On April 4, civil rights leader Martin Luther King Jr. was assassinated while standing on the balcony of a motel in Memphis, Tennessee. James Earl Ray, an escaped convict who had twice been on the FBI's Most Wanted list, was later captured at London's Heathrow Airport. He confessed and pled guilty a year later. Riots erupted in more than a hundred American cities following the assassination.

An eight-day student sit-in began at Columbia University to protest the university's ties to the defense department and its plans to build a gym over neighborhood objections. Within seventy-two hours, students seized five buildings, and six hundred twenty-eight people were arrested. Members of the Students for a Democratic Society, a left-wing extremist organization, took control of one building and raised the communist flag. The incident inspired student unrest on a global scale and marked the beginning of a worldwide student protest against the war that would go on for years.

In a quintessential example of art imitating life, the "Age of Aquarius" was ushered in by the Broadway Musical *Hair*, which opened at the Biltmore Theater in New York and subsequently ran for 1,750 performances.

On June 5, gunman Sirhan Bishara Sirhan shot Senator Robert Kennedy at the Ambassador Hotel in Los Angeles. Kennedy died the next day at Good Samaritan Hospital there.

In Miami Beach, Richard M. Nixon and Maryland governor Spiro T. Agnew were nominated at the Republican national convention. In Chicago, the Democratic national convention nominated Vice President Hubert Horatio Humphrey for the presidency on the first ballot, while police and thousands of antiwar demonstrators clashed in the streets outside the convention hall.

The country seemed to be coming apart at the seams. Because all of the political and social unrest was completely beyond our control, and as we were only going to be in port for a short period of time, the only sensible thing for us to do was to go out and have a good time.

As usual, we found solace in music, and it was a pretty good year for that. The Rolling Stones released "Jumping Jack Flash." Johnny Cash recorded a live concert album at California's Folsom Prison, and it would later be listed by *Time* as one of the 100 most important albums of all time. Simon and Garfunkel sang about "Mrs. Robinson." The Rascals had "People Got to Be Free" and "It's a Beautiful Morning." Otis Redding sang "(Sittin' on) The Dock of the Bay," and Cream sang about a "White Room" and the "Sunshine of Your Love."

All of this music and more was played at the area's three popular discotheques, Picardi's in Waterford, Fiddler's in Groton, and Maybry's at Ocean Beach. We went dancing at least three nights a week, usually hitting all three clubs, and on weekends there was the phenomenon known as the speed run.

In Connecticut during the late 1960s, there were blue laws on the books that regulated the sale of alcohol. On Sundays, bars opened at noon and closed at 9:00 PM, which was all right if you were watching a football game, but if dancing was on your mind, you were out of luck in Groton. However, only 50 miles away in New Haven, home to Yale University, things were different. A club just outside the city called the House of Zodiac opened for dancing at 5:00 PM on Sunday. They had a jacket and tie dress code, and the music was live, usually performed by The Duke, The Duchess and the Magnificents—a soul music big band patterned after Otis Redding and Carla Thomas; they played the best that Motown had to offer. The dress code was never a problem because we were always sharply turned out. Avery and I fancied ourselves to be clotheshorses, and we shopped at a fashionable men's store on State Street called Fedric of New London. This shop catered to doctors, lawyers, and other moneyed professionals, and we bought the best we could afford. All we really had to do was find a ride, and that was never a problem because many of our shipmates had automobiles that they purchased with their variable reenlistment bonuses—and what cars they were! There were European sports cars like Mike Miller's black Mercedes coupe; Rick Obey's green Opel GT, which, with its headlights up, resembled a frog on wheels; and Dick Austin had his red Volkswagen hatchback. There were also muscle cars like Dick Kadlec's Plymouth 440 six pack; "Harvey" Tarr's Dodge super bee 283; Roger Windon's 390 mustang GT; and Ken Schack's 383 Dodge charger. All of these huge engines seemed to idle at sixty miles an hour, and they crossed the Gold Star Memorial Bridge like it was a bump in the road. Any of these vehicles easily carried us to the House of Zodiac, where a roomful of very attractive college coeds waited to dance on a late Sunday afternoon. At 9:00 PM, the club closed, and the evening was supposedly over—but not if you could make the speed run to the

USS *Sturgeon* decommissioning, January 1994. (Author collection)

Dick Bell (left) and Muffy Toland, Shakedown Cruise 1967.
(Courtesy Dick Bell)

Sea-to-sea transfer, Shakedown Cruise 1967 (Courtesy Bill Drake)

Making rate, quarters on the pier, Ft. Lauderdale, 1967. (Courtesy John Fitzsimmons)

The author at El Morro Castle, San Juan, Puerto Rico, 1967. (Courtesy Dick Austin)

USS STURGEON (SSN637)
Care of Fleet Post Office
New York, New York

PLAN OF THE DAY MONDAY 12 JUNE 1967

Duty Officer: LT LORENZEN/LT DAVIS/LTJG WIDHELM Eng Duty CPO: ROSS, ENC(SS)
Duty CPO: ZINGRICH RMC(SS)   Section Leader: LAMOTHE, QM1(SS)
Duty Section: I

Sunrise: 0611 - Sunset: 2028

0645 Breakfast
0730 Breakfast is secured. Up all bunks
0745 Liberty expires for all hands. Muster on Station. Officers and CPO's
      muster in the Crew's Mess
0800 Turn to. Commence ship's work. Officers, CPO's and LPO's assemble in the
      crew's mess
1130 Lunch
1230 Lunch is secured
1300 Rig weapons handling system
1500 Station the weapon handling party for final briefing prior to Safety Study
      and NWAI
1600 Liberty commences by department heads for personnel up to date in
      qualification in Sections II and III to expire on board at 0745 Tuesday
      13 June 1967. Qualification delinquents muster with the Duty CPO.
1730 Supper
1900 Duty section muster in the crew's mess
2000 Qualification delinquents muster with the Duty CPO.
2030 Movie

Upon return to New London, there will be 3 leave periods of 7 days each.

      Arrival 15 Jul - 0800 22 July, 0800 22 Jul - 0800 29 Jul
      and 0800 29 Jul - 0800 5 August

A maximum of 20 people per leave period will be allowed. Turn in requests for
leave prior to Wednesday 21 June so that proper adjustment of dates and reasonable
planning can be accomplished.

Yesterday, a drunken sailor fell from the pier into the river and went directly
to the bottom without ever surfacing. An outstanding job was done by HELMS and
TOLAND in searching for and recovering the body. An additional "Well Done" to
the large number of other STURGEON people who assisted in this operation.

The following personnel are delinquent in qualification: (* those designated by
an asterick will remain aboard until 1200 Saturday)

*BUCHANAN   *EWERT *FITZSIMMONS *GOCHMONOSKY   *LITTLE   *WILSON, T.K.
*TOLAND   *WILLINGHAM *MCKELVEY   BARR   CLEWIS   CORNIBLERT
CASTLE   GARLOW   TARR

SCRIPTURE THOUGHT FOR THE DAY

But the salvation of the righteous is of the Lord: he is their strength in the
me of trouble.
                    W.I.MELTON,LCDR,USN
                                                        Psalm 37:39
                    R.W.LAUTRUP, LTJG, USN
                    Duty Officer

USS STURGEON (SSN 637)
Care of Fleet Post Office
New York, New York
09501

PLAN OF THE DAY THURSDAY 24 AUGUST 1967

0030 Movie: Racambole
0715 Breakfast
0800 Qualification delinquents in Sections 1 and 2 muster with the COW.
1115 Lunch
1200 Qualification delinquents in Sections 1, 2 and 3 muster with the COW.
1300 Wardroom Lecture - BQA-8
1600 Qualification delinquents in Section 3 muster with the COW.
1915 Supper.
2030 Movie: JULIE THE REDHEAD

NOTES:

1. Shoe lockers are for shoes - USE THEM!

2. A lot of valuable equipment is not secured for sea. A heavy roll or large angle with the present conditions would be very expensive. Secure things. We a to "angle and dangle" enroute to NLON.

3. "A" Division personnel are the only people authorized to adjust air condition and heater controls. In cold water improperly set controls and defective heater result in excess condensation.

B. DEMARS
LCDR, USN

Plan of the Day by XO DeMars (Courtesy COB Bill Welsh)

Randy Little (left), appropriately out of focus, and Dan Albright.
(Courtesy Dan Albright)

The house at 83 George Avenue. (Courtesy Dennis Schulz)

Caricature of Captain Shellman by Don Troxel. For the record, Shellman loved it. (Courtesy COB Bill Welsh)

The refrigerator at "83." (Courtesy Dick Bell)

Knickerbocker Café in Westerly, Rhode Island, some seventy miles away on the other side of Groton. At the Knick, there would be dancing until 1:00 AM, and in the summertime, you could also hit the clubs along Misquamicut Beach. Monday mornings we were back on duty on board the boat. Fueled by alcohol and gasoline, these speed runs happened every week, and it's nothing shy of miraculous that no one was ever hurt.

The combination of alcohol and automobiles also led to a series of comic misadventures, always involving the boat's Frick and Frack of the muscle car set: Dick Kadlec and Harvey Tarr. Tarr remembered two such instances:

One night, Dick Kadlec and I were coming from Groton after spending the afternoon and evening at Gino's, watching a football game. The game was quite a few beers long, and we were coming back to the sub base along River Road. It was winter, and the road was in a bad condition, so Dick decided to turn around and go back on the main road. We managed to wind up stuck in the mayor of Groton's flower bed, and sure enough, here comes a cop! We both got arrested . . . he for DWI [driving while intoxicated] and me for public intoxication. Public intoxication! Are you kidding? That was the normal state for most submariners during the Cold War. We beat the rap since no one saw him driving, we were parked when the cop came, and I was not on public property. A good lawyer is sometimes worth the expense!

Another time we were going to sea on a long patrol and I drove my car home to Massachusetts and took the train back to New London. I stopped in Boston and had a few and brought a six-pack for the train ride. When I got to New London, I hit Bank Street for a few more. We were going to sea the next day, and I would be doing without (mostly) for a couple of months. I ran into Dick Kadlec, and after a few more, he offered me a ride back to the boat. As we were leaving New London, a cop stopped us. Dick rolled down the window, and the cop said that he smelled beer. Kadlec points his thumb at me and says, 'He's shit faced!' The cop accepted this explanation and let us go!"

In the words of Bruce Kuykendall: "God blesses fools and sailors, especially submarine sailors."

Tilting at Windmills

It wasn't all fun and games while the boat was in port. There was a lot of work to be done before the fall deployment. Long periods at sea made for a great deal of "catching up" on your return. There was always a mountain of mail, all of which had to be dealt with, and as soon as I made rate, Slack assigned the crew service records to me as my major responsibility, and I became more and more involved in the day-to-day operation of the boat. I learned as much as I could as fast as I could about the Bureau of Personnel and the maintenance of the enlisted service record. In the structured world of the U.S. Navy, there are set procedures for everything, and the smallest of errors in the process would lead to consequences down the line.

The recent change in command structure had given some hope to EM2 Herbert J. Youngquist, who asked me, as the new kid on the block, to rectify a situation ignored since he reported on board. His past requests had fallen on deaf ears. Slack explained that former XO Melton didn't want to deal with it, and he believed that it just couldn't be done. Youngquist contended that his reenlistment contract had been botched by the yeoman at the nuclear power training unit and that he had been cheated out of a significant amount of money that was due him via the variable reenlistment bonus. Bonuses were available to "critical" rates the Navy wanted to retain for more than one six-year enlistment. Nuclear power training was very expensive, and the Navy wanted to get the most out of its investment before men took their expertise into the private sector. Therefore, bonuses were offered to those who would re-up and commit to at least seven years or more. Some of those bonuses were for as much as $10,000, which was a lot of money in 1968. Youngquist received some money, but not what he was due, and he suspected that the yeoman responsible had shorted him intentionally.

This was a real Don Quixote quest. To rectify the problem, we would have to unmake the reenlistment contract and start over, which involved getting BUPERS (the Bureau of Personnel) to admit that a mistake had been made; this was the reason the problem had not been addressed before. A huge military bureaucracy like BUPERS does not like to admit mistakes, and this was a contract that Youngquist had signed. In their eyes, the deal was done.

I sat down and read the manual for reenlistment and then looked at Youngquist's contract. Certainly no expert, it was clear to even me that it wasn't right. I looked at Slack and said, "Let's bring it to the new XO. Maybe he'll be willing to try."

I had Youngquist sit down with DeMars in his office and explain what had happened at the nuclear power training unit. I showed the XO chapter and verse on reenlistment from the BUPERS manual, and DeMars agreed to address the problem. Long letters were composed and sent to Washington, detailing the mistakes that had been made. Initially, BUPERS was unwilling to listen, but after repeated demonstration of the errors, they agreed to review the problem. It took almost a year, but Youngquist finally received his money. This happened because an XO was willing to rectify a seemingly unsolvable injustice—to tilt at windmills—for a fellow crewman. Doing paperwork may not seem like much, but to this day I think that was one of our greatest accomplishments.

The COB

In the summer of 1968, the commissioning crew COB was transferred despite his stated willingness to remain on board. The COB is usually the most senior enlisted man on board a submarine, and as the direct liaison between the commanding officer, XO, and the crew, he is critically important to the operation of the boat. The COB was also one of the first men you met when you reported on board a submarine, and all of the younger guys who reported on board *Sturgeon* had the scars to prove that they had met and worked for Bill Welsh.

From Lawrence, Massachusetts, TMCS(SS) William Welsh, Jr. joined the Navy in March 1945. After boot camp in Sampson, New York, he was assigned to landing ship medium transports in the Pacific, where he rode out the remainder of World War II. After the war, he spent a year at a Naval Air Station in Argentia, Newfoundland. He finally went to submarine school and afterward struck for the rate of torpedoman on board the USS *Diodon* (SS 349), on which he made patrols to Korea and the China Sea during the Korea conflict. In 1953, he transferred to the USS *Corsair* (SS 435) in New London. After ten years of sea duty, he was assigned to submarine school staff. From there, he went to the USS *Skipjack* (SSN 585) and then to *Sturgeon*, where he was one of the first men to report on board as part of the new construction crew. He met his wife, the former Ruth Park of Methuen, Massachusetts, while on emergency leave in 1952. She worked for the Red Cross. They married in 1953 and bought their house in Mystic in July 1960, while Bill was on submarine school staff. They reside there to this day.

Welsh was a great COB. He stood only five feet six inches, but he was tough, and if he told you to do something and you didn't move fast enough to suit him, he'd kick you in the shins to get you going. He did everything a great COB is supposed to do. He stood up for his men, pushed them to make rate, supervised their qualification process, bailed them out of jail, and got reduced punishments instead of captain's masts whenever possible. He worked twelve-hour days, seven days a week throughout the two-year construction process, and he effectively supervised *Sturgeon*'s transition from a new construction boat to an operational boat, including everything we did on the shakedown cruise, the nuclear weapons certification, and the first patrol. He wanted to stay on board because he liked Bohannan, but BUPERS wouldn't allow it. His replacement as COB was a well-liked E-7 nuclear-trained engineman named Homer H. Ross Jr.

Homer

From Salem, Connecticut, Homer H. Ross Jr. joined the Navy in 1952 at the age of seventeen. He went to boot camp in Bainbridge, Maryland, and engineman's school at Great Lakes. After a stint on board the USS *Thuban* (AKA 19), he went to submarine school. He served on board the USS *Trout* (SS 566), USS *Sailfish* (SSR 572), USS *Archerfish* (AGSS 311), USS *Hardhead* (SS3 65), and USS *Angler* (SS 240). He attended nuclear power school in New London at Cromwell Hall, went to upstate New York for prototype duty, and then to USS *Sea Dragon* (SSN 584). After three years of shore duty at Windsor Locks, he was the second man to report on board *Sturgeon*. Bald, paunchy, jovial, and liked by all, he was the boat's Buddha figure, and one of the first things he did as COB was push me to get qualified.

Dolphins

I spent as much time as I could that spring and summer getting signatures on my qualification card. If you fell behind schedule in the qualification process, your name appeared on what was known as the Dink List. The Delinquent Qualification List guaranteed you less liberty and far more time on the boat trying to learn systems. Although I never made the list, my quest for making rate put me a little behind the acceptable timetable, and there had been instances where men were transferred off the boat because of their inability to qualify. However, as a petty officer 3rd class, and one who suddenly held a fairly important position, I started to get a lot more help with the learning process. Doors that had been closed up to this point now opened to me.

There was one word that described those submariners who really knew what they were doing. If you were "heavy," you were knowledgeable. You could be heavy on a particular piece of equipment or a system, or your rate, but if you were "heavy on the boat," then you were truly respected. I took it upon myself to consult with guys who were known to be both heavy on their equipment and heavy on the boat. I needed all the help I could get because, truthfully, my facility with tools did not extend beyond the realm of kitchen utensils.

EN1 Bruce Kuykendall helped me understand the forward half of the boat. Auxiliarymen are responsible for almost everything on a submarine, and Kuykendall had a reputation for being really heavy on the boat. He was also the one man on board who truly understood the complex machinations of the oxygen generator. More affectionately known as "the bomb," the generator was a device that took desalinated and demineralized water and broke it down into the elements of hydrogen and oxygen. Bad things can happen when something goes wrong with that process. I went to Kuykendall because he had a specific approach to helping guys learn the boat: "When young pups came on board, if they had something to offer, and they had interest in stuff, I was going to impart as much knowledge on them as I could."

I was a "young pup" in need of help, and Kuykendall was the man for the job.

At the end of his first enlistment, Kuykendall was stationed on board the USS *Barb* (SSN 596) at Pearl Harbor. At that time, the Navy was sending enginemen and machinist's mates to Swift Boats in Vietnam. Married to his high school sweetheart, the former Donna Lasica, and the father of three small children, he reenlisted for new construction in Groton before the Navy could reassign him to Asia. He reported on board *Sturgeon* in 1965, when there were only 30 men on board. As it was assembled, he learned every inch of the boat and spent his entire second enlistment on board *Sturgeon*.

Nuclear power school graduates like Barry Avery, Ken Schack, Richie Golden, and Harvey Tarr helped me understand the propulsion plant and all other things aft of frame 57. I had different guys give me a series of mock examinations on safety procedures and finally, in

September, my qual card was complete, and I was ready for my walk-through.

A walkthrough is nerve racking, and mine was no exception. The operations officer, Lt. Cdr. Guy Curtis III, presided, along with nuclear-trained EMC Bob Gustafson; HMC "Doc" Kucharski, who was my division chief; and TMCS Cal Johnson, who replaced Welsh and would eventually become the COB. Because I lived most of my life on board in the operations compartment, they were particularly thorough in that area. I stood my underway watch in the control room and slept in crew's berthing Delta in the lower level, and my office was next to the XO's stateroom on the upper level. Fairly heavy on the compartment and its safety procedures, especially the control room, I breezed through that part of the examination with confidence. I was terrified, however, that my mind would go blank and I wouldn't be able to remember anything about the rest of the boat. Somehow, that problem didn't materialize, and before I knew it, the whole thing was over. I passed and was officially qualified in submarines. My relief was palpable. On September 19, the second day of the second northern run, Captain Bohannan presented me with my Dolphins during a ceremony in the crew's mess. Finally, I was a qualified member of the crew and the submarine service.

Polynya Delineation

The 1968 northern run was scientific in nature. Not sent to collect intelligence information, we instead tested equipment designed to ensure safe passage for submarines under the polar ice cap. New sonar could actually measure the thickness and the density of the ice cover. It was all about "polynya delineation." If we could find a polynya—spot where the ice cover was thin enough—then we would surface through the ice.

The search for a northern passage had been around for centuries, and the USS *Nautilus* (SSN 571), under the command of the late Capt. William R. Anderson, made history in 1958 by completing the first trans-Arctic voyage under the ice cap. Ten years later, it was particularly troubling to realize that the top of the world was a potential launching area for a Soviet ballistic missile submarine. However, to do that, the Soviets would first have to surface before they could launch their missiles. Part of our task was to prove that American attack submarines also could successfully operate under the ice cap and thereby pursue their mission of neutralizing the Soviet SSBN threat. The patrol was a success, and *Sturgeon* was awarded her first meritorious unit commendation.

While we were away, the Beatles recorded "Hey Jude" and *The White Album*—their first records under the Apple label. Other 1968 releases included the Rolling Stones album *Beggar's Banquet*, the Band's *Music From Big Pink*, and Iron Butterfly's seventeen-minute classic "In-A-Gadda-Da-Vida." A McDonald's franchise in Pittsburgh sold the very first Big Mac for forty-nine cents. President Johnson halted the bombing in most of North Vietnam, and four days later the country elected Richard M. Nixon and Spiro T. Agnew; in response, students nationwide burned their draft cards on National Turn in Your Draft Card Day. General Motors introduced the first sports utility vehicle, the Chevrolet Blazer. Nixon named Henry Kissinger as his security adviser, and the U.S. stock market began an eighteen-month decline of 44 percent. There is no evidence of a correlation between the two events.

We arrived home in time to witness the infamous "Heidi" game at Gino's, when NBC cut away from the final minutes of a New York Jets–Oakland Raiders football game to begin a television special on schedule. The Jets led 32–29, with one minute remaining. Deprived of seeing the Raiders come from behind to beat the Jets 43–32, football fans across the country screamed in protest.

The year 1968 was bleak. Assassinations, antiwar protests, and riots rocked the nation on land, and death roamed the seven seas. In January, three days after the *Seawolf* ran aground in the Gulf of Maine, the Israeli submarine *Dakar* sank off the coast of Crete. Sixty-nine men died. Two days after that, the French submarine *Minerve* sank off of the coast of Toulon. Fifty-two men were lost. Nearly ninety men died in March when the Soviets lost the *K-129* off the coast of Hawaii, and it was reported they lost another boat in the Arctic. Finally, *Scorpion*, with ninety-nine men on board, sank on May 22. Altogether, close to four hundred men went to a watery grave on board those boats, which represents the greatest loss of life on board submarines in any single year since World War II. It wasn't called hazardous duty for nothing.

Part III

1969
At Our Best

The Greenhouse

IN JANUARY 1969, "Broadway Joe" Namath and the New York Jets defeated the Baltimore Colts, 16–7, in Super Bowl III at the Orange Bowl in Miami. Namath had predicted the outcome.

Richard Milhous Nixon's inauguration as the thirty-seventh president of the United States began what historian Arthur Schlesinger would later refer to as the "Imperial Presidency." Maybe that's why Congress doubled his salary. The Paris Peace Talks began, with Henry Cabot Lodge as negotiator; the *Saturday Evening Post* went out of business; and I made second class. I took the test when we returned from the northern run and passed first increment.

In December 1968 and January 1969, USS *Sturgeon* participated in a series of antisubmarine warfare (ASW) exercises off of the coast of Florida, and at one point in the middle of these exercises, we arrived in Cocoa Beach, Florida. We tied up to a pier at Patrick Air Force Base and hooked up to shore power. The crew, with the exception of the duty section, was put on rest and relaxation. I was in my office, going through the mail, when I heard an announcement on the 1MC: "Yeoman to topside . . . yeoman to topside."

I climbed up the weapons loading hatch to find a representative from base special services. He introduced himself and then told me that because we were here for recreational purposes, he had something that would make our stay in Florida more enjoyable. "What have you got?" I asked him. "Your chief of the boat asked for the Greenhouse. Well, it's all set up for you to enjoy while you are here. Come on. I'll show it to you."

He took me on a short walk to a single-story, cinderblock building set up as a recreation center with Ping-Pong tables, foosball tables, picnic tables, card tables, a variety of board games to choose from, and a bar. He showed us the bar, and next to it was a walk-in style reefer about ten feet long, filled to the ceiling with cases of beer. There was room for one man to walk in, grab some beer, and then walk out. We were to put one man from the duty section behind the bar, and he would charge twenty-five cents for a can of beer. At the end of our stay, special services would come back and collect the money.

"What do I have to do?" I asked. "Sign for it," was the response. "Gimme that clipboard."

So, at the ripe old age of twenty-one, I signed for a building full of beer. The first bartender that night was Larry Scott, a droll nuclear-trained electrician who promptly set the tone for the rest of the week by getting smashed while on duty. It didn't take long for the special services people to realize that they had seriously misjudged our boat's capacity. Bruce Kuykendall remembers, "We were the only boat in, and they gave us the Greenhouse. The word came back that no submarine had ever emptied the building. We did it in a matter of days. They had to fill it two or three times while we were there."

On the way into Cocoa, everyone on board made plans for the first night; everyone except me, that is. I went back aft to see what another denizen of crew's berthing Delta had planned.

Avery

A nuclear-trained IC2 from Oberlin, Kansas, Barry Kent Avery enlisted in the Navy right after high school in 1964.

"I had a brother who was on the USS *Kamehameha* (SSBN 642), and he liked it," Avery remembers. "I didn't really want to go to college. I didn't have the money, and I didn't want to borrow it, so I enlisted."

He attended boot camp and A school in San Diego, or as he put it, "In Tijuana."

The nuclear power training unit in Idaho and submarine school in New London followed nuclear power school on Mare Island. Avery reported on board *Sturgeon* on the shakedown cruise in 1967. He met his future wife, Heather Fenton of Groton, Connecticut, on a blind date set up by Dick Bell's girlfriend Janice. After Bill and Caroline Drake married and moved into their own apartment, Avery moved into 83.

When I asked Avery about his plans for the evening in Cocoa, he said, "Benjamin Edmondson and I are going over to the enlisted man's club on Patrick Air Force Base to drink margaritas. Want to come?" I was in: "Sure."

Off we headed to the enlisted man's club, where, at happy hour, margaritas cost sixty cents. I had never tasted a margarita before that night. It was the beginning of a wonderful week.

For the remainder of our stay, the crew could be found at the Greenhouse, the enlisted man's club, a piano bar called the Mousetrap, or the Cork Lounge, which featured nightly entertainment by exotic dancers. COB Homer Ross remembered, "The guy that ran the Cork Lounge liked us so much that when we showed up, he'd move people off the better tables and give them to us." At the end of the evening, the dancers were invited back as special guests to the Greenhouse, where they were treated like royalty.

The Mousetrap featured a nightly sing along. Everyone participated, but they never expected Thom Keaney, Rick O'Bey, and me.

Keaney

Thomas Edward Keaney of Boston, Massachusetts, enlisted in the Navy in 1965 after receiving a draft notice. He did his boot camp and A school at Great Lakes; nuclear power school in Bainbridge, Maryland; and prototype training at Windsor Locks. He graduated from submarine school in 1968 and reported on board *Sturgeon* on January 13, 1969.

When Barry Avery moved out of 83, Thom moved in. He met his wife, the former Dee Elliott, while in nuclear power school, and they were married in 1970.

O'Bey

Richard Arthur O'Bey played drums in a rock 'n' roll band from southern California called the Deacons. They made several records, and the influential disc jockey Kasey Kasem touted them as a band to watch. In 1965, O'Bey's mother discovered an envelope from the U.S. Army in the mailbox. As soon as he heard the news, O'Bey hustled to the recruiter and enlisted in the Navy. He attended boot camp and A school in San Diego, nuclear power school in Bainbridge, and prototype training in upstate New York. After submarine school, he reported on board *Sturgeon* in 1968. He met the former Angela Costanza of Mystic, Connecticut, in 1970, and they married in 1971.

The three of us liked to sing, especially after a couple of drinks. At the Mousetrap one night, we made the piano player play every old song we knew. We sang solos, duos, trios, Irish songs (Keaney and I knew a lot of those), and anything else that we could get him to play. We were a huge hit until we started to forget the lyrics. As Rick Obey said, "Our career on the piano bar circuit was short lived, but memorable."

Role Reversal

The naval exercises off of the coast of Florida were also memorable. Austin and I became the planesmen in the underwater hull surveillance party, a special watch section comprising some battle stations personnel in Control and Maneuvering. With communications between Control, Sonar, and Maneuvering limited to the sound-powered headsets, and the remainder of the boat rigged for quiet, underwater hull surveillance was one of three special procedures, the others being the missile tracking party and the sound pressure level party that were introduced by XO

DeMars when he reported on board. During those exercises, our crew witnessed Captain Bohannan in a tactical situation for the first time.

The ASW part of those sonar tests turned out to be a nautical version of the fox and the hounds. The surface ships and at least one diesel-electric submarine represented the hounds, all of which were equipped with improved ASW and sonar capabilities. *Sturgeon*, of course, played the part of the fox, and the whole thing turned out to be one-sided because we enjoyed two unassailable advantages: We had our boat, and we had the captain.

The game required us to transit through a specific operations area during a fixed period of time, while the hounds attempted to find us. They never did. *Sturgeon* was supposed to be the prey in this scenario, but Bohannan reversed the roles. He played with them like *Sturgeon* was a cat and they were the prey. On one masterful occasion, we came right alongside the fleet boat, and the captain communicated with them on the UQC (underwater communications set.) Sonarman John Fitzsimmons recalled, "The captain asked them, 'Can you hear us now?' They replied, 'No.' We were so close to them we could actually hear conversations inside their boat! We asked the captain to confirm the range with a single ping. It turned out we were about a hundred yards away!"

We were in and out of port during this time, and scuttlebutt had it that the CO (commanding officer) of the destroyer didn't believe that Bohannan played by the rules. He actually thought that we had not transited through the operations area at all, which was tantamount to saying we cheated. During the next exercise, Bohannan pulled *Sturgeon* directly behind him and then called for the underwater hull surveillance party. As soon as the watch was manned he brought the boat shallow and raised the periscope. The scope had a built-in camera, and Bohannan began to photograph the underside of the ship that was, at this point, directly above us. Barry Avery, who was in the control room at the time, recalled this underwater conversation: "He contacted their

Captain on the UQC. 'Can you hear us now? I'm right underneath you' 'You can't be' 'Of course I can. You're noisy. There's something fouling your port screw that made you easy to find.' 'How can you tell that?' 'I'm looking right at your screw. Looks like a Number Ten can, tomatoes, I think!' 'That's not possible.' 'Sure it is. Go ahead, ping me!'" If he had "pinged" us with his fathometer, it would have indicated that he was traveling in about two feet of water!

For those of us in the control room, it was thrilling. The captain was in complete command of the situation, and he enjoyed it. A year before, this would have been unimaginable. John Kiss, a nuclear-trained electrician's mate remarked, "I never felt so confident about my safety in my entire life." And Ken Schack remembered, "The next time we pulled in, Bohannan took the pictures of the underside of the surface craft with him to the meeting, put them on the table in front of their CO, and said, 'You've got barnacles!'"

In late January, we were getting ready to depart on another sonar operation when Captain Bohannan became ill with pneumonia and was hospitalized at Patrick Air Force Base. The exercise could not be cancelled. When the XO went to the hospital to visit the captain and to see whether he would be able to rejoin the crew and get underway, Bohannan told him he had arranged for DeMars to assume temporary command and take the boat out for the ten days or so that was required. On February 3, 1969, DeMars sent a message to SUBLANT: "Underway with XO in command."

Years later, in his remarks at the *Sturgeon* decommissioning ceremony in Charleston, DeMars would recall, "That was one of the proudest moments in my naval career, and it happened because Bo Bohannan made it happen, and he remains one of my heroes to this day."

Rear Adm. George Davis believes that "it's the only time that happened in the history of the submarine service."

The fact that it did happen speaks volumes about two extraordinary men.

Showboat

Upon completion of the sonar testing, we returned to New London to prepare for another northern run. In the news, President Nixon proclaimed he would end the Vietnam War in 1970. Dwight D. Eisenhower, the thirty-fourth president of the United States, died at Walter Reed General Hospital in Washington at age seventy-eight. "Sergeant Pepper" dropped off the charts after eighty-eight weeks. Simon and Garfunkel released "The Boxer," and Paul McCartney denied rumors that he was dead.

Upon our arrival in New London, one of the first things we noticed was an increase in inspections, and a greater emphasis on formality, all attributed to the new administration. At one point, we received instructions that enlisted men should address each other as "Petty Officer," followed by the man's name. That was greeted on our boat with an unbridled level of ridicule. For a few days, we lived the instruction to the letter until it started to get on everyones' nerves. Submarines have always been less formal than the rest of the Navy. *Sturgeon* was no exception, and the working environment on board such a small command made an instruction like that unenforceable. Eventually, we just ignored it.

One thing we could not ignore was our reputation as a show boat. In March, the Navy decided to use *Sturgeon* as a recruiting poster, so we were scheduled to make a port of call at Annapolis and play host to the entire brigade of midshipmen over a period of four days. Nothing could have been worse. First, there was no place to pull in. Annapolis was built on the shore on the Chesapeake, and the water pierside was not deep enough to accommodate our boat. That meant we could not hook up to shore power, as we normally would. Instead, we had to anchor out in the middle of the river and run the reactor the entire time. We also had to man a topside crew to handle the launches that brought the midshipmen on board for a tour of the boat, and of course, we had to give the tours. None of this pleased anyone. I spent all four days in the control room answering questions from men who called me "sir." It made all of us a little crazy. So, when it came time to go over and see Annapolis, we were ready for the experience. I'm not sure that Annapolis was ready for us.

Truthfully, I don't remember much about Annapolis because I wasn't sober the entire time we were there. None of us were. Even the captain got hammered one night. Thom Keaney had to help him back to the boat. I came perilously close to missing movement when I was late for the last launch back to the boat just before we got underway. Fortunately, they sent another one to bring Dick Bell, Gary Cornibert, and me back at the last minute. That cost us twelve hours of extra duty, which was administered immediately. I stood the maneuvering watch, followed by my own watch, and then twelve hours of extra duty followed by another six-hour watch. Only then was I allowed to go to sleep. I was so tired that I slept every off-watch period for three consecutive days.

We returned to New London and received word that newly appointed secretary of the Navy John H. Chafee had scheduled a visit to the New London naval base, and as part of his tour, he would also visit *Sturgeon*. Because the secretary of the Navy was third in line from the president of the United States in the naval administrative chain of command, this announcement led to the mother of all field days. On the day of his arrival, *Sturgeon* couldn't have been cleaner, and the crew was positioned strategically at their workstations throughout the boat to allow a clear path for the secretary and his entourage to walk through without inadvertently bumping into any of us. That day, the captain, with the assistance of the XO, played host to not only the secretary but also the squadron commanders, the base commander, a couple of admirals, and several other high-ranking members of the secretary's staff. It was the biggest parade of "scrambled eggs"—or officers at the rank of commander or above—I ever witnessed. I was seated in my office, trying to look busy, when the captain and the secretary passed by. At that moment DeMars took the opportunity to point out to Secretary Chafee that I was the boat's "Rhode Island boy." The parade stopped.

John Chafee was a former state assemblyman and two-term Republican governor of the state of Rhode Island, and a member of one of the so-called Five Families—the Browns, Metcalfs, Goddards, Lippitts, and Chafees—who held the state's financial power. They ran the textile mills, the Rhode Island Hospital Trust, the *Providence Journal-Bulletin*, Brown University, the Rhode Island School of Design, and the state Republican party. Basically, they ran the state for hundreds of years. Rhode Island was over 60 percent Catholic and overwhelmingly Democrat, but Chafee enjoyed widespread political popularity and eventually would go on to serve four terms in the U.S. Senate. He would be the first Rhode Island Republican elected to that office in almost fifty years, and in his final election, he carried every city and town, winning with 65 percent of the vote. After his death, a memorial statue was placed in Colt State Park in Bristol, Rhode Island. A good likeness, it portrays him facing north, striding toward the statehouse. Chafee was a true patrician who always brought honor and dignity to the otherwise ignoble profession of politics, and in Rhode Island, he is revered to this day.

At heart, though, Chafee was a politician, and he knew he wouldn't be secretary of the Navy forever. So on that day on board *Sturgeon*, he opened the door to my small office and walked in to introduce himself to one of his constituents. Rhode Island is a very small place. It is marked by one degree of separation, and if I told my family that Chafee had visited the boat, their first question would have been, "Did you meet him?" Chafee understood that about his constituency and was gracious enough to make sure the answer was in the affirmative. We spoke for several minutes. He asked me where I came from and where I went to school, and when I told him, he knew my neighborhood well. He campaigned there years before, and I reminded him of a story that my mother used to tell about serving him a cup of tea. He was a delightful and charming man, and on that day, at that moment, he stopped the world to shake my hand, and in the process, he gave me a sense of pride that I had never felt before.

Goin' North Again

Near the end of April, we headed out on patrol again. We knew we were headed back to where we had been in 1967, only this time Bohannan was driving the boat. As we entered the Denmark Strait, he made this announcement on the 1MC: "This is the captain speaking. We're headed north through the Denmark Strait, and the water temperature outside is approximately thirty-five degrees. If the human body were to be exposed in these waters, life expectancy would be about five minutes. Carry on!"

In other words, if anything happened to the boat on this patrol, there would be no rescue. As Donald Deeter once said, "Just put your head between your legs and kiss your ass good-bye!"

We were only underway for a day or so when the COB informed Fred Davies, Denny Schulz, and me that we would stand junior officer of the deck (JOOD) watches while the boat was on station. We were to man the Mark-19 plotter, a dead reckoning tracker (DRT) that stood just forward of the fire control panel on the starboard side of the control room. The intention was to have three officers in the control room for every watch, and there were not enough junior officers in the wardroom to accomplish that. In addition, the officers stood "four by eights," and with the chart in the hands of someone standing "six by twelves," there would be more consistency to the record.

The Mark-19 was a DRT table with a glass top. Under the glass top was a motor aligned to the ship's gyrocompass. A continuous piece of chart paper stretched across the top of the table, and the light in the motor allowed you to mark the course and speed of the boat. Against that course, you could plot sonar contacts by drawing lines from the boat's position to the bearing of the contact. After a while, the lines would intersect, creating a fan-shaped grouping on either side of the intersect point.

You would then align a speed strip, a clear plastic strip with black lines that represented a specific speed—for example, five knots—to the fan of lines to determine the course and the range of the contact. Bearing rates would be estimated by sonar to assist the plotter in determining the correct solution. It was a reliable, time-tested approach to keep track of everything that would happen while on station. Initially, I had no idea how to do any of this, but with instruction from Lt. Cdr. Donald Tarquin, who was on board for the trip and scheduled to relieve DeMars upon our return, I quickly picked it up. It required an attention to detail that I found very appealing, and the whole idea satisfied my earlier contention that I would be good with charts.

While the enlisted JOODs were on the Mark-19, the officer JOODs usually manned the analyzer at the forward end of the fire control panel. An early analog version of a computer, the analyzer was the most advanced technology available and was affectionately known to all as "Mr. Spock." Similar to all computers, it was only as good as the information it received, and when given bearing rate information, it had a tendency to go off on a tangent and develop fantastical solutions, as we would discover in a real situation later on.

If You Couldn't Laugh About It . . .

I think it was the second day of the trip, and I was at work in the office with YN1 Art Malone, a "legal eagle" who had replaced Tim Slack as the senior yeoman on board. In the wake of the Youngquist incident, DeMars insisted that Slack's replacement have some legal experience. Malone's principal job underway was to type the patrol report. Both of us had Top Secret clearances, but the patrol report was a need-to-know document that would be handled only by him. On this day, however, we were doing routine yeoman stuff when suddenly Emmanuel Howard appeared in the doorway, mad as a hornet!

"Give me a mother-fuckin' report chit! Give it to me! Give to me right now!"

"Whoa!" I said. "What happened?!"

This explosion of profanity from Howard was so outrageous it took us both by surprise, and forty years later it I still laugh when I think about it. Howard, a dignified veteran, and the one man on the boat liked by everyone, ran the wardroom, and because of that, he was not given to foul language. So, whatever had him riled up, it had to be serious. I'd never seen him this angry. Malone and I were desperately trying to muffle our amusement as Howard went on to mumble something about "puttin' him on report. . . . take him to captain's mast!"

The last thing we needed was to have a captain's mast during the first week of a two-month patrol, so I asked Howard to show me what was wrong. We went down to the middle level of the operations compartment, and when we arrived at the door to the wardroom pantry, Howard dragged out an eighteen-year-old steward striker named Griffin, who had reported on board just before we left, and whom I had suspected would be a problem.

"Intelligence is quantified as the global capacity of the individual to act purposefully, to think rationally, and to deal effectively with the environment."[1] The Wechsler Adult Intelligence Scale was published in 1955, and it provided three scores: a verbal IQ, a performance IQ, and a composite IQ score based on the combined scores. The average score was one hundred, allowing for fifteen points above and below as a standard deviation, and this is the range where most adults fall.

The Navy administered a similar battery of examinations to every recruit in boot camp, and the results became part of your service record. The two most important scores were the GCT, or general classification test, and the ARI, a math test. When combined, the GCT/ARI scores were a pretty good barometer for a man's IQ. Most of the men on *Sturgeon* had combined scores that hovered between 120 and 130, and some were even higher. These were smart men; if not book smart, they were still incredibly gifted problem solvers who could fix anything, and they were responsible for the operation and maintenance of one of the most complex pieces of machinery ever invented. Griffin's combined scores were a little above room temperature. He was what the Navy referred to as a "conditional enlistment." By this point, the Vietnam War was so unpopular that the armed services were having trouble filling quotas on a volunteer basis, so in certain nonessential rates, the standards were lowered to allow for better recruitment numbers. How a nonessential, marginally intelligent steward striker who had never attended submarine school ended up on our boat for a two-month patrol was a mystery to me, and yet standing in the passageway in front of me, looking sheepish and forlorn, was what some genius at BUPERS thought was the logical answer to the needs of the Navy as applied to *Sturgeon.*

Howard then said, "Go ahead . . . show him, you dumb son of a . . . !"

Griffin then lifted his trousers to reveal that he was wearing a sock on only one foot. Gary Cornibert, who had the roving IC watch came by, and I grabbed him: "Stay here! I need a witness for this."

I looked at Griffin and asked him where his other sock was. Howard answered for him, "That's just it! He ain't got no other sock! He only got one!"

My response was to ask, "You mean to tell me that you came to sea for a two-month patrol with only one sock!? Not even a pair!? What were you going to do when you did your laundry, switch feet!?" Gary and I found this to be beyond amusing, but Howard wasn't having it. "Yeoman, don't you start no shit now! I can't have this fool in my wardroom."

I said to him, "Howard, relax. I'm not having captain's mast on the third day of a patrol! What good would it do? It won't make him any smarter than he already is. And what are we going to do, bust him down to seaman apprentice? The paperwork won't leave the boat until we get back. By that time, he'll be seaman again. We'll get him some socks. I've got a couple of old pairs that I don't use, and we'll scrounge up a few more. But you keep him under wraps. And you," I said to Griffin, "Don't touch anything you don't know how to operate!"

The whole situation was preposterously funny, but I was struck by the inescapable irony—it had been Howard who had saved me from a captain's mast two years before. As for keeping Griffin under wraps, his battle station was the laundry.

Patrols were marked by long stretches of time where not much would happen, and then a series of events would lead to spurts of furious activity, and with Bohannan as captain, a lot of those events fell under the "white knuckle" category and they could last for hours, and sometimes days. So, the real enemy on long patrols was tedium. Built into the everyday approach to life on board were a series of scheduled and unscheduled events designed to ensure that everyone was always alert. Planned maintenance on equipment, unannounced drills, making rate, qualification, and weekly field days, when the entire boat "turned to" and thoroughly scrubbed the submarine clean, were all designed to combat lethargy.

Food was critical. For the record, it's a moot point that submariners had the best diet in the military. We certainly had the very best that the U.S. Navy had to offer in terms of the raw materials, but what the cooks did with those materials was another thing entirely. Nevertheless, we often had eggs made to order for breakfast and steak or frozen lobster tails for the evening meal at least once a week. Roasts, chops, ribs, and frozen fish were also part of the menu. On one trip, we had frog's legs way too often, so the kibosh was put on them for the future. "Geedunk," or dessert, was a part of every main meal, and "midrats," a light meal of cold cuts, soup, or breakfast pastry was always available for those who were going on or coming off watch at midnight.

The cooks, of course, presented easy targets for abuse. In truth, they performed serviceably more often than not, and sometimes the meals were nothing less than extraordinary. Then again, there was the occasional meal that you just could not eat. For some strange reason, Yankee pot roast, as prepared by Dick Hamilton, was the nadir of our on board culinary experience.

I like Yankee pot roast. It was one of my mother's best meals, and whenever it appeared on the menu I looked forward it. One day, accompanied by butterscotch pudding—another personal favorite—as dessert, pot roast was listed as the evening meal, and I couldn't wait. As a member of the ongoing 1800–2400 watch section, I was part of the first seating in the crew's mess. I could see the dessert sitting in small bowls, all set up to be presented immediately after the main course, which was being served family style. I took a healthy portion of the meat, the mashed potatoes, and the gravy and dug in. It was inedible. The meat was as tough as shoe leather, and the gravy had congealed since its preparation and was unappealing both to the eye and the palate. Still, there was the promise of the pudding—until Bill Drake walked into the galley to pick up his share, which already had a spoon in it for his convenience. He stepped back into the mess and announced, "Here's the geedunk!"

The pudding had undergone a mysterious transformation. It had taken on the consistency and adhesive properties of wallpaper paste and was affixed to the plate. Drake was holding the entire thing aloft, including the bowl, by the handle of the spoon. At that point, we all faced what was known as your basic fair share meal. You took your fair share and disposed of it, and you did that to make sure that it did not reappear the next day, disguised as some strange form of soup.

Soup on board *Sturgeon* was the exclusive domain of our senior ship's steward, Emmanuel Howard. The wardroom stood "four by eight watches," which meant that Howard always prepared a meal for those officers who went on watch at 1600 hours. Invariably, he would make a large pot of soup, and on those occasions when the ongoing and the off-coming watch would choose not to partake of his culinary expertise, the crew would be the beneficiary. This magical experience always happened around 1620 hours. Howard would open the door to his pantry and quickly place the large pot of soup on the chiefs' table in the crew's mess. What happened next was truly amazing. The arrival of the soup was never announced, and yet the word would spread through the boat at the speed of light. Men would get out of bed for Howard's soup! Within fifteen minutes, at best, it would be gone. Howard, quite simply, was the best cook on the boat—bar none. On a dependent's cruise later that summer, he made baked Alaska for the noon meal geedunk. Everyone who was lucky enough to be on board that day never forgot it.

On the 1969 trip, *Sturgeon* also had a resident baker—CSCS Jim Baker, that is—and he lived up to his surname. As the senior cook on board, he assigned himself the midrats meal, and that's when our crew first tasted sticky buns the way they should be made. Everyone on board put on few pounds because of Baker. He made E-9 when we returned, and he deserved it.

We also had our fair share of zany behavior on board. *Sturgeon*'s resident ecdysiast, one Dennis "Phrog" Cloutier, often arrived on his watch station in the maneuvering room wearing nothing more than a well-placed rag he had commandeered from the back aft rag locker. He'd do anything for a laugh.

Organized recreation contributed to the health and well-being of the crew. Card playing was ubiquitous. Chess and checkers tournaments, along with tournaments for pinochle, cribbage, "pitch," hearts, and spades, were scheduled in the crew's mess. Casino night, featuring poker, blackjack, and even roulette, was very popular, and there were always the nightly movies, one at 2000 and one at midnight.

The movies were the bailiwick of the IC gang, and for the first year or so, the responsibility belonged to an IC1 named Julius Winston "Kelly" Metz. Kelly was a bona fide alcoholic, which definitely affected his ability to secure good films for the boat. He would always get waylaid on his trip to special services to pick up the movies, with the result that the best films would already be taken by the time he got there. As a consequence, our crew was subjected to a series of B movies that not even the most knowledgeable of film buffs on board had ever heard of. On the 1967 trip, it was either spaghetti Westerns or French films with subtitles. Metz was so hopeless he couldn't even get the titles correct. The plans of the day for August 24 and 25, 1967, listed the midnight movies as *Racambole* and *Thirty-Two Paces to Baker Street*. The correct titles were *Rocambole* and *23 Paces to Baker Street.* One could argue that this type of error was caused by dyslexia on the part of the yeoman, but I don't think so. On the August 24, the 2000 movie was listed as *Julie the Redhead,* but when the first frames revealed the real title to be *Julie La Rousee* the film was greeted with howls of disapproval. Metz was eventually transferred off the boat, and the responsibility for acquiring films fell, thankfully, to Gary Cornibert. His motto for selecting films was much more in keeping with crew's idea of entertainment: "If it said 4.0 and had lots of skin, I picked it."

That approach often led to selections like *One Million Years B.C.,* a truly awful adventure fantasy that showed men and dinosaurs living on earth at the same time. However, it featured a young Raquel Welch wearing just about what "Phrog" Cloutier wore to his watch station, and for that reason alone, it was a huge hit on board. I thought we would wear out the print.

Practical jokes were always entertaining. On every patrol, a couple of crew members would announce they were going to lose weight—a difficult task at best, especially with Baker on board. They would often give up halfway not knowing that, while they were asleep, their belts had been shortened by other crew members. Some would eventually find out that they'd been had—others wouldn't.

The ugliest beard contest was an ongoing patrol pastime. Everyone just stopped shaving, and at the end of the run, whoever had the ugliest beard was declared the winner. There were no prizes. At the beginning of one patrol, the XO had the idea that we should do away with that contest and be more attentive to our appearance. Just about then, the door to his stateroom disappeared. This was accomplished by anonymous thieves (rumored to be led by machinist's mate Joe Damario), who were determined to hide it where it could not be found. There are not a lot of places on a 637-class submarine to hide something as big as a door, but it was done. The door spent the better part of a week in the fan room, behind the precipitator. Eventually, it was returned in the same manner it was stolen (after all, we were a stealth boat). The XO good-naturedly took the hint, and the ugliest beard contest was officially back on.

Then there was the incident known as the commissaryman's ball. Before we left port, *Sturgeon* failed an efficiency "E" inspection. The reason given was that the oxygen generator was disassembled on the floor of AMR1 (the forward auxiliary machinery room) for maintenance, and the inspectors felt that they could not issue the award with the unit in that state. Weeks later, while underway, someone from the auxiliary division complained about a subpar evening meal to Dick Hamilton, and he snapped back, "Yeah, well, we would have had the efficiency 'E' if the auxiliarymen hadn't dropped the ball!"

That was a mistake. The next day, a strange object appeared in the crew's mess. Hung from the overhead near the clock and the bug juice (a noncarbonated soft drink) machine was a series of metal rings circled around a crumpled-up piece of tinfoil, labeled "CS Ball." The object vaguely resembled a model for an atom, and it functioned as a culinary barometer. The CS ball portion was suspended by a hook and could be removed from its position inside the series of rings to a position at which it hung below the rings to indicate, if the meal was unacceptable, that the commissarymen had dropped the ball. The CS ball stayed in the crew's mess long enough for Hamilton and the cooks to get the message.

On the spring patrol in 1969, I published a newspaper. The idea came from a forward electronics technician named Clewes, who was a very good sketch artist. He was particularly good at recreating the character Snoopy from the Charles Schulz cartoon strip *Peanuts*. By this time, it was well known that Captain Bohannan was likely to turn up anywhere on the boat at any moment. He liked to walk around and visit with men on their watch stations. Ken Schack said, "Every night he came back aft in his tee shirt and talked to a different guy."

Bohannan also smoked a pipe while underway, so the character of Snoopy smoking a pipe was created to represent the captain, and every week while underway, we issued a cartoon that showed him in a different part of the boat. One week he peeped over the reactor plant control panel. The next week he hung off the fire control panel in the control room to observe what was happening on the Mark-19 plotter. Another time he hung off of the periscope behind the diving officer. The cartoon was a huge success, and so was the newspaper, which was yellow journalism at its best—or perhaps its worst. I had a captive readership of over a hundred men, who also served as the paper's reporting staff. Almost nothing was edited out. It was open season on everyone, and dreadful puns were the order of the day. If someone said or did anything really stupid, it made front page news. Poetry, jokes, and sea stories were included, and I published any uncensored traffic that came off the VLF loop (an underwater antenna that received regularly scheduled radio transmissions). Real-world news and baseball box scores and standings were all included.

Many events were reported as though they were part of a page six gossip column. Harvey Tarr recalled several humorous incidents that would have made the news. For example, during the reactor plant start-up before we left, Tarr had the lower-level engine room watch and witnessed the upper-level engine room watch, whom he thinks was Jerry Derryberry, step into an open hatch, fall into the lower level, and land on his feet. Derryberry looked around to see if anyone had noticed, and then scrambled up the ladder as if nothing happened. The newspaper might have asked, "What unexpected social caller 'dropped in' to the lower-level engine room during the reactor plant start-up?"

On another occasion, Dave "Gomer" Garlow used a petcock on the lubricating oil purifier to oil his whetstone so he could sharpen a knife. The petcock malfunctioned and sprayed hot lubricating oil all over Gomer. Fortunately, he was unhurt. The newspaper item might have read, "Who in engineering is the 'really big man in oil' these days?"

Tarr kept a collection of *Playboy* magazines hidden in the 400-pound reducing station next to his rack in the bow compartment. One day the auxiliarymen lifted the relief valve, and the entire collection just exploded. Ken Schack said, "It looked like confetti in there. Tarr was almost in tears!" The newspaper might have reported that as an obituary: "Whose collection of 'fine art' recently succumbed to an exposure to 400 psi air?"

Tarr also provided this delicious in-port observation which actually had happened a couple of years earlier: "What member of the Seaman Gang was observed pumping the Line Lockers before getting underway?" Tarr had left the boat one day and saw SN Don Troxel pumping the line lockers— Tarr didn't bother to tell him that the line lockers were a "free flood" area, which meant that Troxel was actually trying to pump the Thames River!

I also kept a running commentary on what was happening in the control room. One of our hopes on station was to catch up with the Soviet Union's newest submarines, so I wrote short news blurbs that detailed our attempts to find these particular boats and ran them under serial headlines like "Where's Charlie?" or "Yankee Magazine." Because of that, the newspaper became a piece of top secret material, and all copies were eventually destroyed. However, I knew the whole thing was a success after the first week on station, when I walked by the captain's cabin and heard him say, "Yeoman, when's the next edition of the paper?"

On Station

After a two-week transit, we arrived in our area of operation, not far from where we had been in 1967. This time, however, the weather was considerably nicer, and because it was spring, we also had longer periods of daylight. Almost immediately, we began to register contacts, and this time *Sturgeon* did not shy away. On the contrary, Bohannan closed range with any contact of interest to facilitate the gathering of electronic information by the ECM guys and the spooks. The control room became a very busy place.

The captain also engaged the entire crew in the day-to-day operation on station. The veil of secrecy was lifted: What went on in the control room was no longer the purview of just those who stood watch there. Crewmen who stood watches elsewhere were encouraged to visit the control room, space permitting, to experience up close the reason for our deployment. Turnabout being fair play, crewmen who stood watches forward of frame 57 were encouraged to visit the maneuvering room to see how things operated back there. The result was a crew that really came together, and the path from the upper-level operations compartment, through the reactor compartment tunnel, into the AMR2 (after auxiliary machinery room) and the engine room became a well-traveled highway, but like all highways, it wasn't always entirely safe. Steam plant operator Ken Schack recalled, "There was a sonarman who used to come back to check the cavitation lights, and we'd send him back without his pants."

Again, anything for a laugh.

Dennis Cloutier stood watches in the maneuvering room, but he took it upon himself to qualify as a planesman/helmsman and as a ballast control operator, just so he could fully experience the boat, and he was known to spend some of his off time spelling the members of the watch in the control room just for the fun of it. Years later, we agreed that a 637-class fast-attack was the most exciting thing that either of us ever drove.

There were times when several contacts were being tracked at once, and if something really significant happened, the captain would be notified. When Captain Bohannan walked into the control room and relieved the officer of the deck by saying "I have the CON," everyone was alert. In those instances, the control room became a crowded place with the OOD, the JOODs, the XO, and sometimes even the navigator present. Yet it was a joy to see how smoothly everything went. It never seemed to get out of hand, largely because of the working relationship between the captain and the XO. DeMars was the perfect counterpart for Bohannan. The captain's aggressive approach was tempered by the XO's judgment. In the most complex and tense situations imaginable, and there were plenty of them on that trip, DeMars always seemed to have the correct answer, whether it was something as complicated as Soviet naval practice based on information gleaned from past patrols or as simple as a correct sounding based on the charts. They were so good together we referred to them as Batman and Robin.

Alone, Bohannan was better still, with fabulous instincts and the patience of Job. Bill Drake recalled one instance, "We were chasing this contact and we lost him. The captain then ordered 'right ten degrees rudder . . . all ahead full!' We did that full bell over a course of a half hour or forty-five minutes. When we slowed down again, that contact was right there! I mean, he was just amazing."

There was a retractable seat attached to the bulkhead near the number 2 scope for the officer of the deck to sit on, but Bohannan chose to forgo that and instead sat on an empty number ten can that was kept in the control room just for him. I once watched him sit on that can, with his pipe, for the better part of a six-hour watch while we tried to reacquire a very significant contact that disappeared right in front of us. Just as in Drake's story, Bohannan played a hunch, only this time he stayed on the same course and chose to wait it out. He sat for hours staring at the repeater for the sonar. After what seemed like an eternity, there was a single blip on the screen, and the captain jumped up and said, "There he is! Right ten degrees rudder! All ahead two-thirds! Come around to two-five-zero!" Then sonar reported, "CON, sonar. Reacquired contact bearing two-five-zero." The captain responded, "Very well." He had executed the course change before sonar could report the contact. It was brilliant.

His patience paid off time after time. A camera attached to the number 1 periscope broadcast anything the captain could see to a monitor in the crew's mess. It is safe to say that what our crew witnessed never appeared on network television. Bill Drake recalled, "We knew in advance that they had a missile shoot scheduled. We waited two weeks for that. There was a barge loaded with gear . . . antennas, radar . . . all sorts of stuff to measure the speed and trajectory of the missile. When they launched it, instead of going over the barge, it went right through it! Blew a huge whole right in the middle of it!" Richie Golden remembered, "It looked like it was covered in trash can covers, and we laughed when the missile blew the shit out of it!"

The Foxes and the Hounds

I entered the control room one afternoon to find *Sturgeon* on a due east course with multiple contacts, including a couple of Kashin-class destroyers and several Osa-class missile boats, all designed for ASW, being tracked already. It remained unclear as to what was going on, but Bohannan was determined to find out. The Osas traveled back and forth across one section of the ocean at very high speeds, and the Kashins waited in two different areas. DeMars suggested it had all the trappings of a Soviet ASW exercise and that they might run one of their own boats through the operations area in an attempt to track it in a drill not unlike the exercise *Sturgeon* had engaged in earlier that year. In the other scenario, of course, they were all looking for us. Not long after I assumed the watch, sonar reported, "CON, sonar. Possible submarine contact bearing zero-zero-zero."

We tracked the submarine contact on the Mark-19 and on the fire control analyzer, which was operated by a red-headed lieutenant (junior grade) named Hoff. With the boat at periscope depth, the captain observed everything from a distance through the number 2 scope as we continued on the due east course. The bearings from sonar came on a steady basis, and it wasn't long before I had a pretty good solution, when sonar called: "CON, sonar. We believe this contact is a Russian November-class submarine."

An older version of an attack submarine, the November-class boats appeared in the late 1950s. Over three hundred feet in length, and armed solely with torpedoes, they displaced 4,700 tons submerged. Although they were the basis for the Hotel-class missile boats, there was no indication that this particular contact fit that description. It became obvious that this was indeed an ASW exercise, only the Russians didn't know that there were two submarines in the area—two foxes, so to speak. We tracked that November class for quite a while, until sonar reported, "Possible contact 'zig' based on an increase in bearing rate." The captain responded, "Very well. Stay on top of him."

Hoff factored the bearing rate change into his solution on the anaylzer, and I stayed true to the solution that I had, which by this time showed us very close to the contact. Then I heard the captain say, "Mark these bearings. Mark! Mark! Mark! Mark! Mark! Mark!" He spun the number 2 scope around and called out the bearings so quickly I couldn't keep up. They were as much as 20 to 30 degrees apart and made no sense.

"This is a patrol plane flying figure eights. Just draw a big figure-eight pattern around those bearings. What do we have for a solution on the target? What does 'Mr. Spock' say?" From the analyzer at the forward end of the fire control panel, Hoff replied, "The increase in bearing rate indicates a course change, captain. Contact is headed northwest, out of the area."

"What have you got, Yeoman?"

"One-seven-nine, five hundred yards, dead ahead, captain."

"That's him. He's on a one-eight-zero course. They don't have him yet, but we do."

A moment later, the captain again called out "Mark these bearings. Mark! Mark! Mark! Mark! Mark! Mark!" and a second figure-eight pattern overlapped the first.

"Where's the 'X' in the figure eight? Where do the lines cross? That's his target. Where's the 'X'?"

I turned toward the periscope.

"Captain, we're the 'X.'"

"OK. I think it's time I got the hell out of here! Down scope. Right full rudder. All ahead two-thirds. Make your depth two hundred feet."

And with that, we slipped away. No one followed us. The Soviet patrol plane sighted our periscope and must have thought that we were their target. Because we were only five hundred yards away from what they were looking for, they wouldn't have been able to tell the difference until later, when they discovered their guy wasn't at periscope depth. Bohannan snuck inside their nautical playpen, observed the entire operation, came within five boat lengths of what they were looking for, and except for a bit of momentary confusion, managed to evade the best ASW that the Russians had to offer.

Submarine Proctology

Victor-class Soviet submarines first appeared in 1967. Their teardrop shape allowed for speed, and their mission was to protect Soviet surface fleets and attack American ballistic missile subs. Victor-class boats sported six tubes for launching torpedoes, mines, and cruise missiles—an armament that American submarines did not have at the time. Up to 330 feet in length, with a displacement of almost seven thousand tons, these boats were bigger and faster than *Sturgeon*, but not quieter. One day, sonar reported one steaming on the surface. Bohannan called for the underwater hull surveillance party. Kuykendall remembered, "We were walking around in our socks trying not to make any noise. Nobody on board was talking."

Austin and I scrambled to the control room. I took the helm, and he hopped on the stern planes. Ken Schack remembered, "They woke me and told me to get to Maneuvering. When I got there, Homer said, 'take the sound-powered headset.' I put it on and said 'Schack on the line,' and then I heard the captain's voice, 'Don't answer anything I say, and don't answer the engine order telegraph—just do what I say.' After that, the orders were 'Take off four turns' or 'Increase two turns.' I said, 'Captain, what are we doing?' He said, 'Come up after the watch and I'll show you.'"

The captain brought *Sturgeon* up behind the Victor class. We trailed directly behind him close aboard while sonar recorded every sound emitting from his hull. The slightest alteration in course could affect the sound signature, and Bohannan took his time to allow that to happen. We then went a little deeper, and he brought us directly underneath the Soviet boat. He raised the number 1 scope and examined and photographed the underside of its hull. At that point, the captain and I engaged in the most intimate of conversations, conducted just above a whisper as he calmly and methodically altered course and speed.

"Steer two-nine-five."

"Two-nine-five, Aye."

"Two-nine-five and a half."

"Two-nine-five and a half, Aye."

"Take off four turns." He altered the speed of the boat by as little as two revolutions of the screw—an extremely difficult task for the steam plant operator.

"Two-nine-six."

"Two-nine-six, Aye."

"Add two turns. . . . Bring me up a foot."

This time we could do just that. The boat was in perfect trim. With the smallest adjustment of the stern planes, Austin moved our 4,500-ton vessel within inches of another submarine that was half again as big. Bohannan slowly crept his way up one side of that hull and back down the other. The atmosphere in the control room was unlike anything we experienced before. No one breathed very deeply, and tension hung in the air, while the rest of the crew stood silent at their posts. In my memory, this was the single moment on board *Sturgeon* when it all came together: the training, the drills, and our experience on previous operations. Connected viscerally to the captain, our crew no longer just operated the boat—we were the boat.

After what seemed like an eternity, the captain lowered the scope and said, "OK, I'm done with this guy. Right ten degrees rudder. XO, I want to put some distance between us and then get a fast pass with the high-speed camera on the number 2 scope. We'll have to coordinate that as it comes up."

DeMars grabbed a high-speed camera, designed to fit right over the eyepiece of the scope. The action required the scope be raised, the camera attached, the shot taken by the captain, the camera removed, and the scope lowered, all in one continuous motion.

"Come to two-nine-five. Make your depth six five feet."

"Six five feet, Aye."

"Two-nine-five, Aye."

"Bring me up easy, chief."

Moments later, the diving officer, TMCS Cal Johnson reported

"Six five feet. Steady on two-nine-five, captain."

"Very well. Are we ready? Up scope!"

The scope rose, DeMars dropped the camera over the lens, and we heard a whirring sound: click, click, click, click, click, click, click, click.

"Down scope. All right, navigator, plot me a course away from this guy, and let's ease away. Let's not let him know we were here."

All of that activity occurred in the time it took you to read the last two sentences. A few minutes later, we secured from the underwater hull surveillance party, and the normal watch section resumed. Schack remembered, "I went forward after we secured the watch, and he showed me pictures of a hull. I said to him, 'Captain, we had to be very, very close to get these pictures. How close were we?' 'About six inches to a foot.' 'What would we have done if he pulled the plug?' 'We would have lowered the scope and pulled the plug faster.'"

We would have had to—otherwise, we'd have all felt like the inside of a grilled cheese sandwich. On my way to my office the next day, I walked into the crew's mess and poured a cup of coffee. One of the nukes said to me, "Been back aft yet?" I answered, "No. Why?" And he said, "Go back aft before you go on watch." I took my coffee and headed through the tunnel into the AMR2. On the port side, a series of flat panels covered some electrical equipment. This was the largest flat surface on the boat, and we hung a map of the world there to keep track of our location. Next to the map were six eight-by-ten-inch photographs, side by side. When the captain took those shots, we were so close that it took all six photos to encompass the image—the unmistakable teardrop shape of a Victor-class Soviet submarine with two men clearly visible at the top of the sail. One held a cup of coffee and looked straight ahead, the other held a cigarette. Richie Golden recalled, "You could see the cigarette package in his pocket—a pack of *Lucky Strikes*. The guy was smoking *Luckies!*" The smoker's arm extended in our direction as if to say: "What's that over there?" It didn't matter. By the time the other man turned to see what he was talking about, we were gone.

Later that day, D. W. Smith, an auxiliaryman with an authentic rural sense of humor, stuck his head inside my office and said,

"When the 'Old Man' walks into Control, he brings his balls in a wheelbarrow!"

No argument there.

Transit Home

After more than a month on station, we headed home. By then we were running short on provisions. The transit back to New London was always "quiet time." Usually done on a standard bell at about eighteen knots, and at a depth of about four hundred feet, the intention was to keep it smooth, even, and comfortable, which would allow the captain, who had spent the last six weeks completely overextended, to finally get some rest.

Two kinds of officers reported on board our boat. The first, and the best kind, would arrive and immediately search out the most experienced men, as Bohannan did with Kuykendall, to learn the intricacies of what could only be called an extremely complex piece of machinery. I remember when the operations officer Lt. Cdr. Guy Curtis stood his first watch as officer of the deck after transferring from a SSBN. He sat right behind the chief of the watch and asked question after question about how the boat handled and if there were any special characteristics he needed to be aware of, which was the right thing to do on board

Sturgeon. Curtis ingratiated himself with the watch sections and made his on board transition considerably easier. Of course, there were other officers who, on arrival, believed they already possessed the knowledge needed to do anything. This is the story of one of those officers.

The officer of the deck watch rotated in four-hour intervals, which meant that the enlisted section never had the same officer of the deck for their six-hour watch. Every hour or so, we "cleared the baffles." Done near the top or the bottom of the hour, standard procedure was to slow to one third, alter course long enough for sonar to sweep through the area directly behind us, and then resume normal course and speed. We tried to accomplish this without disturbing anyone. One morning at 0400 hours I was at the helm when a newly qualified officer of the deck, who had reported on board just before we left and who up until this moment had been relegated to watches in engineering, ordered in a loud voice, "Right fifteen degrees rudder!" I sat bolt upright in my chair and replied, "What!!?" This was not the response he expected, or even wanted to hear, and he jumped right down my throat: "I said right fifteen degrees rudder!" I tried to argue: "But . . ." There was no discussion allowed: "That's an order, sailor!" COB Cal Johnson, the chief of the watch, who knew full well what the result would be, leaned over and whispered, "Go ahead . . . do it." I jerked the rudder over to fifteen degrees and reported back, "Rudder is right fifteen, sir!"

Sturgeon banked to starboard like an F-15 fighter aircraft and nosed downward, which forced Austin to compensate with the stern planes to maintain depth. It is important to understand that the captain slept on the port side of his stateroom, and this maneuver effectively knocked him right out of bed. A moment later, he stood next to me in a T-shirt and demanded: "What the hell is going on, yeoman?" I answered: "Officer of the deck ordered a fifteen degree rudder angle, captain." He asked me, "What's your speed?" I answered: "Standard bell, eighteen knots, sir." Bohannan then turned to the officer of the deck and said, "GoddamnitBruce!" and stormed back to bed. Lt. Bruce Boyer came over to me and said, "You could have eased that over. You didn't have to jerk it like that." I answered him, "Lieutenant, it wouldn't have made any difference. At high speeds, this boat really responds to large rudder angles to starboard. It is a design characteristic that we've known about since the shakedown cruise two years ago. I tried to tell you that, but you insisted." Boyer sat in his chair and sulked for the next two hours. He's been known as "Old GoddamnitBruce" ever since.

The Cocktail Hour

The consumption of alcohol on board the boat was strictly forbidden by article 112 of the Uniform Code of Military Justice and was punishable by a court martial. That didn't stop anyone from having a drink, and many men clandestinely brought along "a little something" for the trip. It was common practice to save this something for the transit home and to have a nip before you went to bed. Not sanctioned, of course, it was never an issue as long as performance didn't diminish in any way. For those who didn't think ahead, we had a well-disguised still in one of the torpedo room bilges that produced Howard's recipe for Raisin Jack, and there was always the 190-proof gilly. Combined with orange juice and consumed like a cocktail, one ounce of gilly equaled three regular shots of one hundred proof brandy—the doctor even warned us that consumption of gilly could lead to hallucinations.

Sonarman Jim Hartman recalled one particular night on the transit home: "We were playing cards at the chief's table in the crew's mess, and Doc Kucharski walked out of his office, lifted up the lid of the bug juice machine, and poured a pint of gilly into the orange-flavored side. We all thought, 'Well, it's going to be a good card game.' Doc had a little. We had a little. A few minutes later the engineer, Lt. Cdr. Bob Lewis, came out of the wardroom and poured himself some of the orange bug juice. He looked at us and said, 'Bug juice tastes pretty good tonight' . . . and then he walked back into the wardroom. A little while later, the XO came out and had a glass, then the OPS [operations] officer. It wasn't long before the whole wardroom came out to have a bit. Pretty soon, that orange drink was all gone, and only the grape flavor was left behind. No one ever said a word."

Captain Nemo

After two weeks of transit, we surfaced near Point Alpha in the Narragansett Bay operations area. I scrambled up the ladder in the trunk to take my turn in the rotation as a lookout. We arrived at the spot where we usually made the turn to head up into the Race, and there we encountered a new Soviet ploy to disturb American submarine activity. Stretched out before us were five Russian fishing trawlers, right in a row. Although they looked like fishing boats, they weren't really trawlers. Obviously spy ships, they all had dozens of antennae to gather electronic intelligence. One was larger than the other four and was obviously the mother ship. The ships sat right on the three-mile limit and waited for American submarines. Their position obstructed our passage. However, a Man of War has the right of way on the high seas, and Captain Bohannan was not about to let a bunch of poorly disguised Russian spies stand in his way: "Right ten degrees rudder. All ahead full!"

He pointed *Sturgeon* on a collision course with the mother ship. Our speed increased, the nose of the boat dove deeper, and water began to splash right up underneath the fairwater planes. I remembered an old Disney movie of Jules Verne's *Twenty Thousand Leagues under the Sea*. In the film, Captain Nemo, played by James Mason, commanded the *Nautilus*, and at one point he turned his submarine into a battering ram. That's what *Sturgeon* must have looked like at that moment, as she knifed through the water, because those trawlers scattered in front of us like bowling pins, and as we passed through the opening, dozens of little cameras clicked away in a Russian Kodak moment.

Gladness and Sadness

Sturgeon moored at pier ten, and I stood topside and watched the captain walk across the gangway with an armful of charts. On his way to brief SUBLANT and the other powers that be, he took charts created on the Mark-19 plotter by Davies, Schulz, and me. He also took copies of the newspaper with him and included them as part of his briefing.

On arrival, I received a Western Union telegram that announced the death of my mother's brother Joseph. Ravaged by cancer at the age of 51, my Uncle Joe was one of the most important people in my life. Every year my brother and I would go on vacation with him, his wife Dottie, and my cousins Tom and Brian. It was never an opulent vacation but, rather, an adventure—camping in the woods of Smithfield or a couple of weeks in a house on cinder blocks by the river in Riverside, Rhode Island—and it was always wonderful. Not a rich man, Joe was one of those guys who never really had two nickels to rub together, but he knew everyone, and when you went anywhere with him, he always made you feel like you were someone special. At the end of each vacation, when he walked all of us into Asquino's restaurant in East Providence, you would have thought he was the king of Siam. He passed away while we were "on station," and because the Navy never allowed that kind of information to be sent to anyone on patrol, I only found out about it after we docked. My heart broke when I read the news, and I miss him to this day.

Emmanuel Howard arrived home to discover his fifteen-year-old son Vance hospitalized after being hit by a car. COB Cal Johnson pulled me out of my office in the afternoon, and the two of us went to Howard's home in Navy housing with some money that had been cobbled together by donations from crew members and what was in the slush fund. Mrs. Howard graciously accepted the assistance.

On board *Sturgeon*, change was once again in the air. Lt. Cdr. Donald C. Tarquin relieved Bruce DeMars as XO, but before he left

DeMars informed me that for my performance as JOOD on station, I would receive a citation from the Commander Submarine Force in the Atlantic Fleet. Schulz, Davies, and others were also honored. Because the patrol was classified, the citation was awarded in a private ceremony. My parents drove from Rhode Island to see Captain Woods, the commander of submarine development group two, present the award at the squadron's headquarters. I didn't realize it, but that moment marked the apex of my time on *Sturgeon*: My days on board were numbered.

After the award ceremony, I brought my parents up to 83. They wanted to see the apartment and meet the other guys who lived there. At that point, Austin, Avery, Schulz, and I were the occupants, and all of us were home that day. Once in the apartment, I introduced my folks to Avery and Schultz. My father then asked to use the toilet. He emerged from the bathroom with a confused look on his face and said, "There's a guy in there takin' a bath and drinkin' a beer!" In unison, all three of us replied, "Oh, that's Dick." Austin took long bubble baths, and always with a beer.

We arrived home in time to witness history. On July 20, we sat in the living room of 83 and watched on a black-and-white television set as astronauts Neil Armstrong and Edwin "Buzz" Aldrin made the first successful landing of a manned vehicle on the moon. Later that night at the Dolphin, we celebrated "one small step for man, one giant leap for mankind."

While back home, the Woodstock Music and Art Fair opened in upstate New York. Over four hundred thousand young people gathered at Max Yasgur's dairy farm in the Bethel hamlet of White Lake, New York, to hear Joan Baez; Crosby, Stills, and Nash; Creedence Clearwater Revival; the Grateful Dead; Jimi Hendrix; the Who; Jefferson Airplane; Janis Joplin; Santana; Canned Heat; Ravi Shankar; and many more performers over a period of four days. None of us went—the greatest assemblage of rock 'n' roll talent in history was, of course, off-limits.

Bermuda

September brought a port of call in Bermuda. *Sturgeon* had pulled into Bermuda twice before, and both of those visits were marked by adventure. At the end of the shakedown cruise in 1967, a large group from the crew, led by "Tommy Two Bellies" O'Neal, descended on the Hog Penny Bar in Hamilton. Harvey Tarr remembered O'Neal: "When the boat was underway, O'Neal would talk about almost anything or almost nothing. He could go for hours, days, weeks, months and never seemed to repeat himself! A world-class bullshitter!" The Hog Penny never knew what hit them.

We returned to Bermuda in February 1968 after the Gulf of Maine incident, and Bill Drake recalled how, on that visit, submariner ingenuity solved an access problem: "We had civilian clothes with us, and we went to a club in Hamilton, but you couldn't get in without a tie. I think it was Randy Little who had an ascot. Randy went in, went up to the second floor and threw it out the window for the next guy. I think ten of us got in on that one tie."

The 1969 trip, however, was at the end of yet another ASW exercise that involved several vessels, including the USS *Skate* (SSN 578). When several commands arrive at a specific port, there is always a SOPA (senior officer present afloat) who implements rules for behavior, especially if it's a foreign port. During this ASW operation, we took the opportunity to exchange movies with the other boats. *Mister Roberts*, a film famous for a scene where a drunken sailor drives a motorcycle off the end of a pier, made the rounds. The SOPA feared, and rightly so, that someone on board one of the boats would feel inspired to do the same, and so moped rental on the island was strictly forbidden.

On Labor Day weekend, we pulled into the military base, away from the town of Hamilton. Our first stop, the Bermadoo Club, sold happy hour margaritas for sixty cents. Even better, our stay in Bermuda was augmented by the arrival of no fewer than five cruise ships into Hamilton harbor, and hundreds of women disembarked from them for the weekend—we had arrived in paradise.

On the last night, several of us returned to the boat late. We were just about to go below when, in the distance, we heard this high-pitched motor. We looked at each other and said "No!" We waited, and sure enough, a sailor on a moped appeared, and he was headed for the end of the pier, pursued by military police and several other witnesses who didn't want to miss the show. A wooden gangplank connected the concrete jetty to the end of the pier. The driver got to the end of the pier, dismounted, walked the moped over to the jetty, put it up on the kickstand, hopped back onto the seat and opened the throttle as wide as it would go. About twenty people ran down the pier after him. He kicked the stand away, and when the tires hit the concrete they propelled him maybe two feet over the side. He went straight down into the water to the sound of laughter and applause on the pier. The moped sank, and the rider disappeared. He swam away, avoided the military police, and snuck back on board his boat.

The morning of our departure, we received word that *Sturgeon* would have a passenger on the way back. IC3 Jack Girnus remembered, "I rode the *Sturgeon* back from Bermuda. . . . I missed movement. Got thrown in jail for too much partying in Bermuda, and the *Skate* left in the morning before I was able to get to court. We had some ROTC guys on board, and they met me in court and paid my fines, and I caught a taxi back to the base. I was IC3 at the time. I came walking down the pier, and my friend SK3 Gary Henry had the topside watch. He and I went through submarine school together. I remember him saying, 'Oh, so you're the guy!' I reported on board to the XO and the COB, and they told me if I was an excellent sailor they would come to my captain's mast back in Groton. Then they told me I was going to mess cook on the ride back. To make a short story here, I was perfect, and they did come to my captain's mast and spoke very highly of me. It was kind of a strange ending. I was standing on the dock in Groton when *Skate* came in. The *Sturgeon* beat them back by a day!"

Jack was lucky. He had hopped a ride on a great boat with a great crew: When we arrived back, *Sturgeon* received her second meritorious unit commendation.

Dark Times

After the Bermuda trip, however, things turned to the dark side. The U.S. Army admitted to the 1968 Vietnam massacre of civilians at My Lai and announced an investigation of Lt. William Calley for the murder of at least a hundred people. Later found guilty and sentenced to life imprisonment at hard labor, Calley was the only person ever charged in connection with My Lai. He claimed that he was a scapegoat who only followed orders. In 1971, President Richard Nixon ordered him released from prison and placed under house arrest, and finally a federal judge threw out all charges against him and ordered him freed. The charges were reinstated on appeal, but he never went back to prison.

The Beatles released their final album *Abbey Road,* and John Lennon called it quits. The Rolling Stones released the *Let It Bleed* album and then staged a rock concert at the Altamount Speedway in Livermore, California, for some 300,000 fans. For some inexplicable reason, they hired the Hell's Angels motorcycle gang for security. One person was stomped and stabbed to death by a Hell's Angel during the show, another man drowned in a nearby canal, and two people were crushed to death by a runaway car; all of it was captured on film for the 1970 documentary *Gimme Shelter*. Suddenly, music wasn't fun anymore.

In September, President Richard Nixon ordered the resumption of bombing in North Vietnam, and I received my 1-A card. I'm not sure which made me feel worse. In the Navy, a 1-A card announces your impending transfer to another command. Just like Bob Bristol before me, I made second class, and there was no billet for a second class on board *Sturgeon*. We kept the news of my promotion quiet for the better part of the year, but eventually BUPERS found out about it, and that was it for me on the 637. The Navy assigned me to the USS *Dogfish* (SS 350), a World War II–era diesel electric fleet boat. The only yeoman on board, I would have my own boat, which at my age was a bit of a compliment, I suppose. The transfer was scheduled for the beginning of the New Year, so I rode out the last few months of 1969 on board *Sturgeon* while she prepared for another deployment in the spring. I wanted to go on that deployment, and I asked the XO to intervene, but yeoman was not a critical rate, and the needs of the Navy were better served with me on board *Dogfish*.

Perhaps my request to stay on board wasn't approved because I wasn't as clever as Bruce Kuykendall. In October, the XO scheduled some retraining for the crew on a Saturday, and no one on board could be excused without a very good reason. Kuykendall knew full well that if he could get a morning off, there would be no way he would come back for the afternoon. So he put a chit in to the XO that said "My shotgun is going hunting Saturday morning from 0745 until 1200. I would like to go with it." Tarquin approved the chit with a note saying, "you make a beautiful couple."

The day of my transfer was also a Saturday, and I went on board in the morning to check the mail before transferring myself off the boat. Just as I was about to go, Lt. Bruce Boyer and ST2 John "Fitz" Fitzsimmons showed up in my office. Scheduled to get out of the Navy in a couple of weeks, Fitzsimmons was "short timing," but his father had taken ill, and Boyer wanted to know if there was anything I could do to help Fitz get home earlier. During my time on board *Sturgeon*, I had developed a reputation for finding ways to bypass official red tape—known as to cumshaw—so I agreed to get Fitz out of the Navy.

The usual procedure involved a transfer to the submarine base, where you would then be kept for menial duties over a two-week period while the submarine base yeomen approached your paperwork at a snail's pace. We looked on this as punishment for having the temerity to leave the Navy. The submarine base looked on it as a source of labor. I sat down, broke out the BUPERS manual, and spent the rest of the afternoon discharging John Fitzsimmons from the Navy. I walked him around the base, through a physical examination, filled out every form, got all of the necessary signatures, and at 1800 hours, when I handed him his orders and his service record, he was, for all intents and purposes, out of the Navy. All he had to do was get the duty officer on the submarine base to sign off on the orders and he could fly home. At the time, I thought it was my greatest accomplishment as a yeoman. I then walked across the gangplank and left *Sturgeon* for the last time. Years later, I found out that the duty officer on the base refused to sign off on Fitzsimmons' papers and he was consigned to cleaning the chief's quarters for two weeks while his father languished in a hospital. And the Navy wondered why we all got out!

Part IV

━━━

1970
Transfer and Separation

The "Dogboat"

THE USS *Dogfish* (SS 350), a guppy II modified Balao-class diesel-electric boat under the command of Cdr. J. M. Conway, was attached to submarine squadron eight. Commissioned in 1946, the boat was older than I was, and at that point it was consigned mostly to coastal patrols. When I reported on board that January, I was unprepared for the prospect of an extended patrol on a fleet boat. The XO, a lieutenant commander named L. P. Cheshire, took one look at my record, saw the two meritorious unit commendations and the citation from SUBLANT, and placed me in charge of the fire control party in the wardroom during the boat's upcoming NATO operation. When I asked, "A fire control party in the wardroom, sir?" he told me that's where the torpedo firing solutions were developed. I knew there was no DRT in the wardroom, and I couldn't imagine how this was done. I asked him, "Who else is in this fire control party?" He answered, "The chiefs." I said, "You mean I'm going to be in charge of a roomful of chiefs?" and he replied, "That's right." Aside from perhaps the captain and the XO, I apparently had more real tactical experience than most of the crew, including the junior officers in the wardroom.

I left the XO's office, found the COB, and told him that under no circumstances did I want to be in charge of a roomful of E-7s and E-8s. As far as I was concerned, he was the boss. He told me not to worry about it.

A week later, we left on a short five-day trip. For the first time in over two years, I found myself without a maneuvering watch station. I thought the best thing to do was to just go lie down and stay out of the way. I climbed into my rack above a Mark-14 torpedo in the forward room, heard the klaxon sound twice, and "Dive, dive" on the 1MC. The boat took a significant down angle, and to my amazement, water roared into the compartment from the torpedo room hatch! I hopped out of my rack, and TM1(SS) Dennis Blado, the watch in the forward room, contacted control. The planesmen reversed the "bubble" and brought the boat back above the waterline long enough for Blado to secure the hatch. We then continued the dive. I thought to myself, "I am going to die on this relic!"

Things calmed down after that, however. The *Dogfish* may have been an old boat, but the crew was a good bunch of guys, and I settled in pretty well. In April, we deployed for a thirty-day NATO operation in the North Atlantic with the British, the French, the Germans, the Dutch, and the Canadians, with Halifax, Nova Scotia, as a port of call at the end in early May. I had never been there before, and I looked forward to that. However, none of us anticipated the one problem we would all have to deal with underway.

We weren't at sea more than ten days or so when one of the crewmen, a machinist's mate 1st class whom everyone called "Ski," had a nervous breakdown. A former reservist, he told me before we left that in the previous fourteen years, he had never been on a trip that lasted more than five days. I found that hard to believe, but with all of the coastal patrols going on, I suppose it was possible. The moment Ski realized he was going to be gone for at least thirty days, he shut down and walked away from his watch station. Dennis Blado recalled, "I had the keys to the gun locker. Ski came up to the forward torpedo room and said he wanted to go home now. I said, 'Yeah, Ski, we are all ready to head home.' He said to me, 'Give me the keys to the gun locker so I can get a gun and shoot the captain, and we will be going home now.' He was serious. I called the COB and the gun boss up to the forward torpedo room, and they took Ski into the wardroom to talk. I am pretty sure we handcuffed him to one of the torpedo skids until he settled down."

Ski was immediately relieved of duty, sedated, and confined to the after battery. A watch was placed on him until we reached Halifax. He then sat in the crew's mess and listened to "A Day in the Life" by the Beatles for twenty-four straight hours. The next day, the cooks put a stop to that before they went crazy as well.

In the interim, the NATO operation continued. The first time I heard "battle stations," I hustled to the wardroom, where I found several chiefs and a bunch of charts. I still could not imagine how we were going to come to a firing solution without a DRT, but the COB said he would show me how they did it. We barely got the chart on the table when we heard "Secure from battle stations." It was clear to me that this was a waste of time, so I went back to the XO and asked if he could find a better use for me in the control room. I volunteered to qualify as a planesman, but he said I was "too senior." Instead, I was placed on junior officer of the deck watches in the conning tower. I found myself monitoring an antiquated sonar repeater that looked like it belonged in the Smithsonian, while a reserve lieutenant (junior grade), who was as nervous as a cat, swung around on the periscope as we snorkeled. At that moment, I realized the metamorphosis was complete: I had gone from standing JOOD watches in the control room of a sophisticated, ultraquiet, technologically advanced "shooter" to standing them in what, by comparison, could only be called a "target."

Snorkeling on the *Dogfish* was a complicated procedure that took a long time to set up. The boat had four batteries and three General Motors "Jimmies" diesel engines with a Prairie-Masker system—a high-capacity 30-psi blower and motor that supplied air to a system of small tubes welded to the circumference of the exterior hull. When the boat snorkeled, the small holes in these tubes emitted an envelope of bubbles around the hull, which lowered noise emissions. However, this feature required one engine to supply power to the blower motor, thereby limiting the charge to a one-engine rate, which meant that it took much longer to charge the four batteries. Once the charge began, you did everything possible to finish it before shutting down. You never wanted to shut down before that, unless it was an emergency. On the NATO operation, there were "sides" to the exercise. I suppose it was that realization, combined with bits of an overheard conversation in the control room between the captain and the XO, which led that reserve lieutenant to believe, despite a lack of visible contacts and no reported sonar contacts, there actually was something closing in on us. I could see that he was overreacting, but I just wasn't fast enough to stop him from calling an emergency shutdown. The diesels went offline, the boat went silent, and the captain had a fit. We then began the long process of reestablishing the snorkel. After that, I convinced the lieutenant to calm down a bit, to take a deep breath, and let me relieve him on the scope periodically. The snorkel wasn't back up and running more than fifteen minutes, and I was hanging on the scope, when I heard something from the control room below. I looked at the lieutenant, and I could see in his eyes that he was going to shut it down again. This time I beat him to the communicator and called below, "Control, CON . . . repeat that last transmission please." The response came, "CON, control . . . there was no transmission." I looked at that lieutenant and quietly said, "You're panicking. Stop it."

I thought he was going to pull rank on me, but he didn't. He knew I was right. Frustrated with that officer, with being on such an old boat, with the "needs of the Navy," with everything, it all seemed an exercise in futility. Instead of traveling north on the *Sturgeon* to play the game for keeps, I was stuck in the conning tower of an archaic vessel and playing make-believe with a panic-stricken ROTC "ninety-day wonder," a product of three months of Officer Training School. I wanted to tell that lieutenant that anything he did really wouldn't have made any dif-ference if a *Sturgeon*-class fast-attack boat was out there. I wanted to tell him that only a year before, *Sturgeon* eavesdropped on conversations inside the pressure hull of an identical fleet boat from only a hundred yards away and remained undetected. I wanted to tell them all that if we were up against the *Sturgeon* herself, the only thing the *Dogfish* was ever likely to hear would be the sound of a Mark-37 torpedo heading right up our ass! But I didn't. They wouldn't have believed me. They, too, were submariners and were proud of their boat, and in their hearts was "Diesel boats forever!" They didn't realize that the submarine world had already changed and that technology had not only passed them by but had rendered them obsolete.

We secured from the snorkel, and I went back down into the control room. As I passed Captain Conway, he said, "You stand a good watch, yeoman."

Dogfish pulled into Halifax, Nova Scotia, at the end of the operation, and Ski promptly ignored his restriction to the boat and put himself on liberty. When I told the XO, he said, "Go after him!"

So, like a spy in some cheesy novel, I followed Ski around the city for hours until he finally returned to the boat. He was then put on a helicopter that took him back to the submarine base hospital in New London. After that, I went on liberty.

With sailors from all those different countries attempting to communicate, the Halifax enlisted men's club sounded like the Tower of Babel. I swapped hats with a guy from Germany, drank very heavy stout with the Brits, and marveled that the Dutch spoke better English than some of the guys on the *Dogfish*. On Sunday, May 10, I watched Bobby Orr score a goal in overtime to beat the St. Louis Blues for the Stanley Cup. It was all the more sweet because the Canadian sailors were Montreal fans. The next day, the newspaper featured a photo showing Orr flying through the air a moment after the puck went into the net. In New England, it is still called "the greatest hockey photo ever." Unfortunately, other news that week proved disturbing.

At noon the previous Monday, May 4, at Kent State University in Ohio, some two thousand students gathered peacefully to protest the invasion of Cambodia. National Guardsman sent by the governor ordered them to disperse, dispensed tear gas, fixed bayonets, and marched into the crowd. A small group of guardsmen then inexplicably discharged their weapons at a group of students, killing four and wounding nine others. Student strikes nationwide erupted in protest. Hundreds of colleges shut down, and over 100,000 demonstrators marched on Washington, D.C. Contrary to eyewitness testimony, photographs, and later investigations, the National Guard never admitted any wrongdoing. Instead, they contended they were provoked. No guardsman was ever punished.

I overheard one man on *Dogfish* react to this news with, "Served them right. Fuckin' Hippies!" and he meant it. Not everyone on board *Dogfish* felt that way, but that response staggered me. Right then and there, I knew I could no longer stay in the Navy. I could not serve with men who believed that innocent college students should be shot for exercising their constitutional right to protest. I had to get out.

Before that realization, I had investigated the possibility of reenlistment in exchange for overseas duty. I made several inquiries and applications, but the answer was always "reenlist, and then you can put in for transfer." I knew enough to understand that this meant nothing. Because my rate wasn't critical, my chances of getting the kind of duty I really wanted were almost nonexistent. I would never again have what I had on board *Sturgeon*, and for the remainder of my time, I would just have to serve the needs of the Navy on board a fleet boat. It suddenly became all too clear that the adventure was over.

Hitching a Ride

That summer, I enjoyed one final nostalgic *Sturgeon* moment. One day, on the lower base in New London, I ran into my old friend Emmanuel Howard. He had been transferred to submarine development group two and now was Captain Woods' personal steward. Howard came up to me and said, "Hey yeo! How're you doin'? Say, listen. I need a ride. I need to get my sub pay. Can you get me a ride?"

The concept of providing additional pay for men serving on board submarines was introduced by presidential executive order after Theodore Roosevelt hitched a ride on board the USS *Plunger* (SS2) in August 1905. "According to newspaper reports, President Theodore Roosevelt slipped away from his home at Sagamore Hill during a driving rainstorm to take a ride on the *Plunger*. The demonstration included diving to a depth of forty feet and remaining submerged for half an hour while the President examined the boat. This was followed by an exhibition of porpoise diving. At one point, all the lights were extinguished and the crew worked the boat in total darkness. By all accounts the boat rested motionless at a depth of twenty feet while a storm raged on the surface."[1]

Before that presidential excursion, not only was service on board a submarine considered shore duty but the men were paid 25 percent less than their surface ship counterparts. Roosevelt deemed that to be discriminatory and inappropriate. He declared submarine duty to be "hazardous and difficult," and he believed that submariners "have to be trained to the highest possible point as well as to show iron nerve in order to be of any use in their positions."[2]

In the late 1960s it was common practice for shore-based submarine personnel to continue to receive submarine pay by riding along on short trips on board fleet boats attached to squadron eight. You only needed a couple of days at sea every month, and Howard, with his large family, was a man who needed that money. I told him, "Sure, Emmanuel, I'll get you a ride." I went back to my boat and asked the XO how he felt about "riders." His response was clear: "No riders."

It took me the rest of the week to convince Cheshire that he really wanted this particular rider. I promised that Howard would not just hang around and do nothing. I said that on one night, he would spell the cooks and prepare a meal for the crew. The rest of the time, he would

work in the wardroom. Cheshire finally gave in and agreed to take
Howard on as a rider. Howard agreed to the terms, and the following
Monday, just before we "singled up" the lines, he reported on board for
a five-day trip.

As promised, Howard worked in the wardroom all week, and one
night he cooked the evening meal for the crew. Despite having the night
off, the cooks ragged me a bit—Howard's pork chops were a hard act
for them to follow.

Dogfish then returned to New London and, for the remainder of my
time on board, resumed weekly coastal patrols. Just before every departure the XO came up to me and asked, "Does Howard need a ride?"

Last Days

For the remainder of my time, I grew to enjoy going to sea on board
Dogfish. The short runs were easy, and I liked most of the crew. Besides
Halifax, we made ports of call in Key West, Florida, and a July 4 week-
end call in Edgartown, Massachusetts, on the island of Martha's Vine-
yard. I would never have seen any of those ports on board *Sturgeon*.
She was too new, too classified, and her draft was too deep.

At Martha's Vineyard, we anchored in Edgartown Harbor and conducted tours of the boat for the locals, while those on liberty ferried
back and forth to town. One contingent from the crew displayed their
patriotism when they gave up part of their liberty to march in the local
parade. They made that decision on their own, without any input from
the wardroom. I stood on the sidewalk as they marched by. They looked
great, and when the parade watchers greeted them with applause, they
beamed with pride.

Another experience unique to fleet boats happened on a return trip
to New London. Without warning, the captain announced "Swim call!"
on the 1MC. That would never happen on a new fast-attack boat. It was
a step back in time: *Dogfish* at all stop on the surface, and lookouts with
M-16 rifles posted up in the sail for shark protection as the crew dove

off the lowered bow planes into the warm, clear waters of the Gulf Stream. Had the moment been recorded on film, it could easily have been a scene from *The Silent Service*—the television show that inspired me to volunteer for submarines in the first place.

I transferred to the submarine base for separation on August 10 and reported to the head yeoman in the base office. He was going to put me to work on service records for two weeks before they would eventually get to mine. I couldn't bear the idea of being in that office for any longer than I had to, so, I looked around, saw a two-foot stack of service records on one desk, and said to him, "What's that?" He answered, "Records waiting to be processed for separation or discharge."

Because I had discharged John Fitzsimmons (or at least I thought I had), I understood the process and knew exactly what needed to be done. I said, "I will process all of those records for you and my own, if can I get out by Friday." He took me up on the offer: "Deal."

It was my last cumshaw in the Navy. By the afternoon of Friday August 14 I was gone.

Less than two years later, *Dogfish* was decommissioned and stricken from the Navy list. She was sold to Brazil in July 1972 and commissioned as the *Guanabara* (S-10). Ten years later, she was scrapped.

In the category of all things must pass, the *Sturgeon*-class attack boats were finally phased out after twenty-five years of service and replaced by the faster, quieter *Los Angeles* class. LA-class boats, however, were not nearly as comfortable, which led some submariners to invoke the saying, "Give me heaven or a 637!" Today, the new *Seawolf*-class boats are reported to be not only the fastest boats ever but quieter underway than the *Los Angeles*–class boats are when tied next to a pier!

After I got out, I went to work in the shipyard. A guy I used to tip elbows with at Gino's restaurant worked in the Electric Boat employment office, and he got me a job doing yeoman work in the SSBN overhaul division. The office was full of retired submariners including Carl Bryson, a survivor of the USS *Squalus* incident.[3] It was mindless work that had already been done by someone else. I had no direction, and no idea what I wanted to do with the rest of my life. I thought about going back to college, but I just wasn't ready to leave the area. I stayed in Groton for another year and celebrated with all of my *Sturgeon* friends as they, one by one, got out of the Navy, got married, and moved away. Toward the end of 1971, I came to the realization that I had hung around too long. So I moved back to Rhode Island. In the fall of 1972, at the age of twenty-five, I enrolled at Rhode Island College, where I studied theater and English. I moved to New York in 1977 and have lived there ever since.

Part V

Looking Back

Denny Schulz (left) and Dick Austin outside 83 George Avenue. (Courtesy Bill Drake)

The water tower at Electric Boat. (Reprinted with permission from *Electric Boat Corporation* by James S. Reyburn. Books available from the publisher online at www.arcadiapublishing.com or by calling 888-313-2665.)

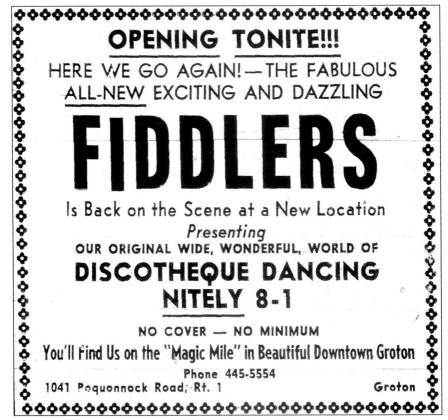

Fiddler's advertisement from *The Day*, the local daily newspaper. (Courtesy *The Day* archives, *The Day* Publishing Company, New London, Conn)

COB Bill Welsh,
Shakedown Cruise 1967.
(Courtesy Bill Drake)

The diving trainer on the sub base. (Reprinted with permission from *Naval Submarine Base New London* by David J. Bishop. Books available from the publisher online at www.arcadiapublishing.com or by calling 888-313-2665)

"The Greenhouse," Cocoa Beach, 1969. Left to right: unidentified, Ron Shinn, Wally Vertz, Dennis Cloutier, Dick Bell. (Courtesy Bill Drake)

"Ugliest Beard" contestants Harry Heineck (left) and Bill Drake. I think Harry won. (Courtesy Bill Drake)

Dennis Cloutier (left) and Thom Keaney. (Courtesy Dennis Cloutier)

The Commissaryman's Ball. (Courtesy Dan Albright)

The cocktail hour, berthing Delta, 1968. Left to right: Avery, Austin, Schulz, Drake, and McHale. (Courtesy Bill Drake)

The author receiving SUBLANT citation from Captain Woods, COMBSUBDEVGROUP II, 1969. (Author collection)

USS *Dogfish* (SS350). (Courtesy USS *Dogfish* Web site, http://www.ussdogfish.com)

The Builder and the Driver

FOR MANY YEARS, security classifications restricted any public discussion of what we actually did on submarines during the Cold War, but thankfully, much of that changed with the Freedom of Information Act. As a stealth boat, USS *Sturgeon*'s primary purpose was to seek out and destroy enemy submarines and other forms of shipping and to conduct underwater espionage against the Soviet Union. She made four extended deployments from 1967 through 1970. The first, under Captain Shellman, was undistinguished. For the other three, under Captain Bohannan, *Sturgeon* received two meritorious unit commendations and one naval unit commendation, and the captain received the legion of merit twice.

The industry standard for nuclear submarine intelligence gathering was set in 1967 by Captain Kinnaird McKee on board the USS *Dace* (SSN 607), and to say there was an unspoken competition among other operational submarines to better that record would be an understatement. Among those captains who successfully operated at that time were Chester M. "Whitey" Mack of the USS *Lapon* (SSN 661), Alfred L. Kelln of the USS *Ray* (SSN 653), and Guy H. B. Shaffer of the USS *Greenling* (SSN 614). Mack achieved great success in the late summer of 1969 when he successfully trailed a Soviet Yankee-class submarine for over 40 days. I've often wondered whether it was the same Yankee class that *Sturgeon* contacted while on station earlier that summer.

Basically, there were two kinds of attack submarine commanders: those who were conservative in nature and followed standard procedures, and those who developed a reputation for more aggressive approaches to gathering intelligence. Shellman was certainly one of the former, and Bohannan was one of the latter. Both men were about the same age and had comparable service backgrounds when they assumed command, but that is where the similarities ended. Shellman was cautious, quiet, and socially uncomfortable. Bohannan was confident, communicative, at ease with anyone, and—like the more celebrated "Whitey" Mack—he fit the mold of the captain who sometimes blurred the lines between aggression and what some considered reckless behavior.

The post-*Sturgeon* career paths of both captains also differed dramatically. Shellman went on to a distinguished career in the Navy, and an even more distinguished career in the private sector. In April 1968, he assumed command of the gold crew of the USS *James K. Polk* (SSBN 645), where his cautious approach to command proved successful during four Polaris patrols. After the *Polk*, he was appointed commander of submarine squadron ten, served on the staff of the chief of naval operations at the Pentagon and retired as a rear admiral. He then went to work for Electric Boat and played a leading role in the improvement of the shipyard's performance. EB delivered eighteen 688-class submarines and eleven Trident-class boats during his term as the head of shipyard operations. Bruce DeMars believes that Shellman would have become the president of EB had he not died of a heart attack in 1990. DeMars said, "He was one of the pioneers of the nuclear submarine program, and his entire adult life was one of service to his country."[1]

James E. Turner, the vice president and general manager of Electric Boat, was quoted as saying that Shellman, "built and maintained a reputation for himself and the division as the best builder of submarines in the U.S. The performance of the U.S. submarine fleet is in large part attributable to his efforts."[2] Shellman was a misunderstood workaholic, whose real legacy was his engineering expertise in submarine new construction. It is part of an enviable safety record. The United States has not lost a submarine since 1968, while in the same period, the Soviets have lost four that we know of. All the incidents involving American submarines that have taken place in the interim have not been the result of any form of engineering failure but, rather, errors in seamanship.

Bohannan's post-*Sturgeon* career is modest by comparison. As captain, he made three fine spec ops, but a collision with a submerged Soviet sub on his final *Sturgeon* patrol in 1970 led to subsequent assignments at shore commands rather than a first-tier major command at sea. After *Sturgeon*, Bohannan went to the staff of the chief of naval operations, became the chief of staff for commander, submarine group eight in Naples, Italy, and from there took command of the naval underwater systems center. At the end of the decade, he retired from the Navy and worked as a consultant for several defense contractors.

Despite the obvious differences in the career paths of these two men, Bohannan was, by far, the better attack-boat skipper. Robert A. Hamilton, a reporter who writes on military matters for *The Day* of New London, published an article entitled "With Rare Exceptions, Sub Skippers are Confident, Stellar Performers."[3] In the article, Hamilton listed the following requisites for being a good submarine commander:

Technical competence tops anyone's list of characteristics for a good submarine CO. . . . Personal integrity. He is going to lead the ship into dangerous situations—that's the nature of his job—and he has to have the confidence of his crew. . . . A skipper must have confidence in himself. . . . A skipper must have physical and mental stamina because there will be long periods without sleep in stressful situations, such as sitting off a coast to do electronic surveillance while enemy surface craft try to find you, or tailing an unfriendly submarine that has ventured within firing range of the United States. . . . A submarine skipper must be both a cheerleader for the crew, and its disciplinarian. He must be the symbol of ultimate authority, but approachable by everyone on the ship. . . . A submarine captain

must demonstrate proficiency in engineering, seamanship, navigation, tactics and the almost indefinable ability to make people follow
him, to bring out the best work of every sailor on the crew.

Using these criteria leads to an interesting, if inevitable, comparison
of two capable, but very different, officers. A more in-depth analysis of
these two men I will leave to the naval historians of the future, who by
then may have access to still-classified material such as patrol reports,
deck logs, and charts.

Both Shellman and Bohannan were technically competent men of
uncompromising personal integrity. Both were confident in their abili-
ties—otherwise, they would never have survived the daunting command
selection process. Both had the necessary physical and mental stamina,
and both were good navigators and engineers, with an advantage to
Shellman in the latter area. However, seamanship, tactics, approachabil-
ity, and the confidence of the crew all go to Bohannan. Shellman maintained a distance from his crew, and as a cautious tactician, he never
inspired the confidence of his men. In the spring of 1967, Lt. George
Borst recalled that he was under a lot of pressure to extend his military
career because Shellman wanted him to be part of the crew for
Sturgeon's first patrol later that fall: "Right after the commissioning, I
had a decision to make. I had to decide if I wanted to go to sea for two
months with Curt Shellman as the commanding officer, and the answer
to that question was no."

Bohannan's leadership, in contrast, remains untarnished in the eyes
of his enlisted crew. In every situation that we encountered, both on station and off, he was always in complete control. Everything he did was
natural, as though it was an everyday affair. A study in confidence, certain that he had not only a superior boat but a superior crew as well, he
made us all believe we could do anything, and in the process, he
brought out the very best in every one of us. Harvey Tarr's friend EMC
Bill Gibbs captured it perfectly when he said this about serving on submarines: "That's the best we ever were—or ever will be."

The research for this book put me in direct contact with many of the men I served with on *Sturgeon*. All of our conversations eventually came around to Bohannan, especially if the men served on board during the change of command in 1968. I asked them to remember something specific about each captain. Shellman, like his initial Executive Officer Melton, remains unpopular in the memories of the enlisted crew, but hindsight and time have tempered once-harsh criticisms to an acceptance that he was a competent, if distant, officer who was better suited to the command of an SSBN. Opinions of Bohannan remain constant, regardless of undersea collisions or the seemingly unfavorable comparison of subsequent career paths. With reasonable certainty, I feel that I can speak for my shipmates. If the enlisted crew of the USS *Sturgeon* in the late 1960s had to go to sea all over again, and like the whalers of the 19th century we were allowed to choose our captain, to a man, we'd go with Bo.

The XO Factor

In the midst of any equation comparing Shellman with Bohannan, there is one variable that cannot be ignored. The template overlapping the confluence point in the careers of those two submarine commanders is the executive officer they shared, Bruce DeMars, and his influence on both of them is undeniable. DeMars brought badly needed spec op experience to Shellman's wardroom in 1967 and changed the XO's approach to everyday life on board *Sturgeon* from parochial to professional. In 1968 and 1969, DeMars' judgment and experience tempered Bohannan's aggressive tactical approach, and the result was back-to-back meritorious unit commendations. Transferred off the boat in the summer of 1969, DeMars was not on board for the underwater collision during Bohannan's 1970 patrol. By the early 1970s, there had been so many submerged collisions during spec ops that submarine school created a three-day program called predeployment training that taught crews how to trail Soviet submarines without collision. DeMars was serving on the submarine school staff at the time, and he instituted the program. In the end, it was DeMars who proved to be the stealth factor in the early success of a stealth boat.

Similar to Kinnaird McKee, DeMars was one of those officers who were apparently singled out for great careers. After *Sturgeon*, he went on to become the first commanding officer of the USS *Cavalla* (SSN 684), commander of submarine squadron twelve, and deputy director of the attack submarine division in the office of the chief of naval operations. As an admiral, he served as commander of the U.S. naval forces Marianas/commander of U.S. naval base Guam, and commander in chief Pacific representative for Guam and the trust territory of the Pacific islands. He went on to be deputy chief of naval operations for submarine warfare and director of the naval nuclear propulsion program, becoming only the third man to hold the office created by the legendary Hyman G. Rickover. He replaced Kinnaird McKee. That program included some 176 reactor plants on over 150 ships and submarines, eight land-based research and training reactors, eight nuclear-qualified shipyards, two Department of Energy laboratories, and an extensive commercial supplier base. He directed the transition of this enterprise to the post–Cold War period and was instrumental in the design of the *Seawolf* and *Virginia*-class attack submarines. When he retired in October 1996, after 44 years in the Navy, both houses of the Congress passed resolutions honoring him for his long service to the nation.

Charleston, 1994

AT THE USS *Sturgeon* decommissioning ceremony on that cold day in January 1994, Admiral DeMars spoke of our service during the Cold War:

All of you served during a momentous period in the history of our country, the Cold War. We won that war. Did we make a difference? Yes! Because of the nature of submarining each and every one of you contributed.

We countered the Soviet navy submarine force's every move. As they got quieter, we invented a towed array sonar and changed our tactics. When they went deeper and faster to compensate for lack of stealth, we modified our torpedoes to go deeper and faster, and we let them know we did it. When they deployed to the Mediterranean in the 1960s, we followed. When they went to the Indian Ocean in the 1970s, we followed. When they went under the ice pack to escape detection, we increased our Arctic deployments from one sub per year to three or four per year.

The Soviets made their submarine force the centerpiece of their post–World War II naval expansion, but we hounded them unmercifully. They always came out second best. Reacting to the pressure of our attack submarines, the Soviets had to commit vast resources in pursuit of undersea superiority—or at least parity. Finally, their system went broke financially and politically. *Sturgeon* was in the forefront of one of our country's most successful Cold War competitive strategies.

Being a submariner is not an easy business. Cramped living, no privacy, hot bunking, everyone stands watch, no idlers, drills, studying, qualifications, extended sea deployments, no mail, no fresh vegetables, etc., etc. . . . It is a young man's business. You are all members of a fraternity of . . . men who each for a period of several years devoted yourselves to USS *Sturgeon* . . . young, hard-working, idealistic men who performed notably under arduous conditions. We can all be proud.

Denouement

MY FOUR YEARS in the U.S. Navy coincided with one of the most interesting periods in the history of the submarine force, the ascendance of nuclear submarines and the decline of the diesel-electric boats. In the beginning of my service, I reported on board the newest commissioned nuclear-powered attack submarine in the fleet and subsequently made her first three patrols. At the end, I made a patrol on board one of the oldest diesel-electric boats in the fleet before she was decommissioned and stricken from the list. I am very happy that I served on board both vessels. The first was the future in the present tense, and the other was the past. As the future, *Sturgeon* was the major, defining experience of my life, and as the past, *Dogfish* gave me perspective—a tangible sense of submarine history—and completed my immersion into a mystique that only those men who have served on submarines can ever truly comprehend.

Years after my discharge, while my father was still alive, we had one of those truth-telling sessions that you inevitably have with your parents. He told me that I broke his heart when I quit Providence College back in 1965. I explained to him that if I had continued on that path, I would have graduated in May 1968 as a second lieutenant in the U.S. Army, four months after the beginning of the Tet Offensive. At that

[153]

point in the conflict, "Second Looeys" in Southeast Asia had a fifteen-minute life expectancy. Instead, I served on board a great boat with a great crew—a vessel whose motto was "First in her class, finest in the fleet." I remain convinced that quitting college probably saved my life, and that the submarine service provided me with not only the first and, perhaps, finest adventure of my life but also the experience and the friendships of a lifetime. I wouldn't have it any other way.

Epilogue: Afterlives

Dan and Judy Albright live in Land O' Lakes, Florida. Dan continues to work as an engineer but is looking forward to retirement.

Dick and Debbie Austin live in Spokane, Washington, where they are enjoying their grandchildren.

Barry and Heather Avery live in Granby, Connecticut. Barry is an engineer, Heather is an accountant, and they are enjoying their grandchildren.

Dick Bell is back in Carson City, Nevada. He and his wife, Lori, are accomplished scuba divers, and every year they travel to a different place to dive. Dick continues to work as a home builder.

Captain Bohannan and his wife, the former Lillian S. Silver of Havre De Grace, Maryland, live in Gales Ferry, Connecticut.

John Buchanan and his wife, Jennifer, live in Lakeland, Minnesota. John is a freelance photographer and owns a half interest in a garbage company in Duluth. He calls his Web site (http://www.johnville.com) the "Home of the 6 Greatest Grandchildren on the Planet!!!!!"

Gary and Lois Cornibert live on Long Island, where they are enjoying their two granddaughters.

Navigator George Davis retired from the navy as a rear admiral. He and his wife, Sara Nell, live on the Olympic Peninsula in Washington, where he is exploring his passion for music as a member of the Bainbridge Chorale.

Adm. Bruce DeMars lives in Alexandria, Virginia, with his wife, the former Margaret Ann Milburn of Chicago. They have two children and three grandchildren.

Bill and Carolyn Drake live in Norwich, Connecticut. Carolyn retired from the Norwich public school system, and Bill retired from UPS. They are enjoying their grandchildren.

John Fitzsimmons retired from a career with Lucent Technologies and is living in Redmond, Oregon. He told me, "If I knew that my professional career outside of the Navy was going to be as unexciting as it was, I might have stayed in."

Richie Golden lives in Colorado and runs a company called Engineering Management.

Jim Hartman went the limited-duty officer route in the Navy and then got out to form his own company, doing research for the Navy. His hobby of working with leather paid off when he was hired to make the gun leather for the movies "Tombstone," "Lonesome Dove," "Wild Bill," and "Wyatt Earp." He and his wife live in the high desert of California near a town called Victorville.

Emmanuel Howard retired from the Navy and then went to work as the head chef at the enlisted club on the New London submarine base. The club never had it so good. Now completely retired, he lives in Groton, Connecticut.

Thom Keaney made a deal for overseas shore duty in exchange for reenlistment. He served in Morocco for three years, then was picked up for two years by the Advanced Degree Completion Program in Washington, D.C. He then served on the USS *Thomas Jefferson* (SSBN 618) and the USS *Queenfish* (SSN 651), where he made chief and was accepted to the limited-duty officer program simultaneously. He was transferred to the USS *Enterprise* (CVN-65) as an ensign for two years and then to SUPSHIP (shipbuilding, conversion, and repair) in New London. After that, he served on the USS *Fulton* (AS11), then with development squadron 12 on the submarine base. At his retirement ceremony in 1995, I sang the national anthem as he was "piped over the side" of the USS *Nautilus*. He currently works for DDL OMNI Engineering, LLC. Thom is married to the former Dee Elliott and they live in Norwich, Connecticut.

John Kiss lives in Stonington, Connecticut, with his wife, Heather, and works as the test coordinator for Northeast Utilities/Millstone.

John Kuester, USN (Ret.), works for RFD Global Solutions, Inc. He and his wife, Linda, live in Penn Valley, California.

Bruce Kuykendall left the Navy at the end of his second enlistment to work for Treadwell, the company that manufactured oxygen generators. After a short time there, he worked for the submarine directorate from March 1976 until he retired in March 1995. He ran performance monitoring teams for the naval sea systems command. On his retirement, the head of the submarine directorate awarded him the Navy Meritorious Civilian Service Award, one of the highest awards that can be offered to a civilian by the military. The citation reads, "In recognition of your sustained outstanding service to the Submarine Engineering Management, Monitoring and Fleet Support Program Office . . . in keeping with the greatest traditions of the Naval Submarine Service. Your leadership and devotion reflect great credit upon you as an individual truly deserving the Navy Meritorious Civilian Service Award. Congratulations on a job well done!" If anyone deserved that, Bruce Kuykendall did. He and Donna are retired and enjoying their grandchildren. They live in Heathsville, Virginia, on the Chesapeake and, in a complete accident of fate, only thirty miles from Hank Marquette.

Hank Marquette lives in a tiny Virginia town on the Chesapeake called Hardyville, where he is known to travel around on a three-wheeled motorcycle called a "trike."

Lin "Mac" McCollum was a Teamster for over thirty years and is now retired and living in Red Bluff, California.

Lt. Dennis Moritz resigned his Navy commission, put himself through medical school, and then joined the U.S. Army as a thoracic surgeon. He retired as a colonel and is now in private practice in Huntington, West Virginia.

Rick and Angie O'Bey live in Newport, North Carolina. Rick is the president of Sunbelt Business Brokers in Morehead City, North Carolina.

Tom and Betty O'Neal recently celebrated their fortieth wedding anniversary. Tom is retired now. He and Betty built a modular home on land next to their grandkids in Peachland, North Carolina, and they split their time between there and Charlotte.

Homer Ross lives in retirement in Colchester, Connecticut, in a house that he built with his father.

Ken and Marianne Schack live in Framingham, Massachusetts. Ken has worked as an engineer for Stone & Webster since he got out of the Navy in 1972.

Dennis and Pat Schulz live in Willoughby, Ohio, where Denny is currently getting his master's degree in special education.

Lt. Rick Shreve got out of the Navy and had a career on Wall Street at Morgan Stanley. He now teaches business at Dartmouth.

Lt. Cdr. Donald C. Tarquin went on to command the USS *Drum* (SSN 677). After the Navy, he founded a company called Sargent Controls & Aerospace, which supplies precision hydraulic control components to commercial and military aircraft as well as all U.S. Navy nuclear-class submarines. He is retired and lives in Arizona.

Richard Harvey Tarr got out of the Navy in 1972. He is currently a consulting engineer for the South Texas Project (STP) Electric Generating Station about ninety miles southwest of Houston, Texas. STP is a 1,250-megawatt electrical power station. The pressurized water reactor is the same as on the *Sturgeon,* only larger.

Bill and Ruth Welsh live in retirement in the same house in Mystic, Connecticut, that they bought over forty years ago.

Author's Note

WHEN I WAS BORN, I was named for my father's brother, who died in World War II when his merchant marine ship was torpedoed by a German U-boat. I was christened William Joseph, and all through my boyhood my family called me Billy. In high school, it was Bill, and in the Navy I was known as Mac or Bill. When I joined the Actor's Equity Association, which is the union of professional actors and stage managers, there already was someone named Bill McHale on the books, and the union did not allow for any duplication. So I had to change my name for professional purposes. Since I am the product of a marital relationship between a woman named Gannon and a man named McHale, I chose my mother's maiden name and officially became Gannon McHale. It made sense to me.

As Gannon McHale, I've enjoyed a modest journeyman's career. I have been privileged to appear on Broadway, off-Broadway, and in a number of the better regional theater companies across the country. I have also toured extensively, appearing on stage in forty-five of the fifty states, including Alaska and Hawaii; all of the western provincial capitals of Canada; four countries in Europe; and two countries in Asia, including a twenty-nine-city tour of Japan that was the cultural experience of a lifetime.

Through the years I have had somewhat of a multiple identity as far as my names are concerned. I answer to all of them. If I'm addressed as Gannon, then it's someone I met since I moved to New York thirty years ago. If someone calls me Billy, it's usually a family member. If I hear Bill, it's someone from high school or college, but if I hear someone yell out "Hey Mac!" you can bet money that it's a shipmate from the Navy.

Acknowledgments

From the USS *Sturgeon* (SSN 637)

Capt. William L. "Bo" Bohannan, USN (Ret.), CO
Adm. Bruce DeMars, USN (Ret.), XO
Rear Adm. George W. Davis VI, USN (Ret.)
Lt. Cdr. Thomas E. Keaney, USN (Ret.)
Lt. Richard S. Shreve IV, USN
Lt. George T. Borst, USN
ET1 Daniel Albright
SK2 Dick Austin
IC2 Barry Avery
EN2 Dick Bell
ETN2 John W. Buchanan
MM2 Bill Drake
QM2 Harry G. Dunn III
ST2 John Fitzsimmons
EM1 Richard Golden
ST1 Jim Hartman
SD2 Emmanuel Howard, USN (Ret.)
EM2 John Kiss

STS1 John Kuester, USN (Ret.)

MM1 Bruce Kuykendall

MMC Herman H. Marquette, USN (Ret.)

SK1 Lin "Mac" McCollum

EM2 Richard O'Bey

ENC Homer Ross Jr., USN (Ret.)

ET1 Ken Schack

ETR1 Thomas E. O'Neal

FT2 Dennis Schulz

MM1 Richard Harvey Tarr

TMCS William Welsh Jr., USN (Ret.)

From the USS *Seawolf* (SSN 575)

MM1 Al "Chauncey" Leach

TM2 Richard Northrup

From the USS *Dogfish* (SS 350)

TM1 Dennis Blado

EM3 Dennis Gallant

MM2 Tam Graham

EM3 Bob Kunze

IC2 Bill Nisbet

EMC Thomas Striffler

From the USS *Skate* (SSN 578)

IC3 Jack Girnus

Thanks to Ron Jones, Web manager, Internet Projects, from the National
Oceanographic and Atmospheric Administration's National Weather Service, for the technical definition of a state ten sea (e-mail dated December
20, 2006).

Thanks to Leo Facchini, athletic director of New London High School, for information regarding the high school track career of Curtis B. Shellman (e-mail dated April 30, 2007).

Thanks to Tom Cutler, Susan Corrado, Christine Onrubia, and everyone else at the Naval Institute Press, and to my copyeditor, Anne L. Hicks, ELS.

Special thanks to Dawn A. Marcoccia for encouragement and support, and to MM1 Dennis R. Cloutier.

Notes

Part I 1965–67 From Jacket and Tie to Bellbottoms

1. Working topside in rough weather on any submarine is very dangerous. On December 29, 2006, four sailors from USS *Minneapolis-St. Paul* (SSN 708) were washed overboard in bad weather as the submarine left Plymouth, England. Two died, including the chief of the boat.
2. http://AmericanHistory.si.edu/Subs/Weapons/Armament/other/index .html.
3. http://www.ibiblio.org/ebooks/Irving/Sleepy/Irving_Sleepy.htm.

Part I 1968 Change of Command

1. When a submarine is traveling submerged and it encounters an abrupt change in water temperature, the boat can react as though it has bumped into something. Thermal layers can also alter the trim of a boat and provide a natural barrier from sonar detection.

Part III 1969 At Our Best

1. http://cps.nova.edu/~cpphelp/WAIS-R.html.

Part IV 1970   Transfer and Separation

1. http://www.geocities.com/gwmccue/Documents/Roosevelt.html.
2. http://larryshomeport.com/html/subpay.html.
3. While on a test dive on May 23, 1939, the USS *Squalus* (SS 192) sank in 243 feet of freezing water near the Isle of Shoals off the New Hampshire coast. Twenty-six men died, but thirty-three survivors were recovered from the forward end of the boat in the most celebrated submarine rescue effort in history.

Part V Looking Back

1. From an article by Maria Helman published in *The Day*, November 30, 1990
2. Ibid.
3. First published August 12, 2002, in *The Day*.

Glossary

1MC: The communication system that could be heard throughout the boat.

A school: After boot camp, a trade school that would teach you the basics of a particular rate. Some of these schools were as long a year in length.

Aft of Frame 57: Frame 57 marked the entrance to the reactor compartment.

AMR: The auxiliary machinery room. On USS *Sturgeon*-class boats, there were two. One was in the lower level of the operations compartment, and the other was aft of the reactor compartment.

ASW: Antisubmarine warfare

attack submarines: Also referred to as a fast attack or a hunter-killer. A submarine whose primary purpose is to seek out and destroy enemy submarines and other forms of shipping. During the Cold War, they were used extensively to conduct underwater espionage against the Soviet Union.

auxiliaryman: A member of the A gang. On nuclear submarines, they were non–nuclear trained machinist mates or enginemen who made up one of the most important divisions on the boat, and on *Sturgeon*, every single one of them was just a little crazy.

BCP: The ballast control panel. The watch station where everything on board can be monitored. A very important position in the control room.

boat sailors: Submariners

boatswains mate: On surface ships, the rate responsible for all things on deck. Originally, on board sailing ships, the boatswain was in charge of a ship's anchors, rigging, colors, deck crew, and the small boats.

boomers: Fleet ballistic missile submarines, or the men who serve on them.

bosun's mate: Same as boatswain's mate

bubble: The up or down angle of a submarine underway. A "zero bubble" is an even keel. Just think of a carpenter's level.

bug juice: A noncarbonated soft drink, like Kool Aid.

BUPERS: The Bureau of Personnel in Washington, D.C. A monolithic bureaucracy.

busted: To receive a reduction in rate and pay. Dcctci was busted from second class all the way to torpedoman seaman.

capstain: A rotating spindle that applies force to lines on board a ship. Used on submarines to aid the line handlers as the boat ties up to a pier.

Captain's Mast: Nonjudicial punishment authorized by article 15 of the Uniform Code of Military Justice. In the Navy, it is administered by the commanding officer of the vessel.

channel fever: Anxiety, usually registered while waiting to tie up to the pier after a long deployment.

Charlie class: In 1969, one of the newest Soviet submarines.

chickenshit: The enforcement of regulations . . . just because you can.

close aboard: Very near another vessel. In fact, closer than you can, or would want to, imagine.

CO: The commanding officer.

COB: The chief of the boat, the senior enlisted man on board a submarine, and the CO's and XO's liaison with the crew.

cocked: Intoxicated, inebriated, drunk, feeling no pain, hammered, screwed up, smashed, snockered, shit-faced, fucked up, and FUBAR (fucked up beyond recognition)

COMSUBDEVGROUP II: Commander, submarine development group two, a submarine squadron in New London.

cumshaw: Pronounced "comshaw"; to trade services for goods, or vice versa.

To skirt normal procedures to achieve a goal in a speedier and more efficient manner. To avoid or bypass red tape.

day hop: A commuter student. A student who does not live in a campus dormitory.

deck gang: Line handlers during the maneuvering watch, and men who worked directly for the chief of the boat. Also known as the seaman gang.

Denmark Strait: The body of water that separates Greenland and Iceland.

diving officer: Supervisor of the dive station. Oversees the helmsman, the planesmen, and the ballast control panel operator. Responsible for the trim of the boat. Usually a chief or a non–nuclear trained commissioned officer.

drag line: A rope attached to a diver.

"drink your dolphins": A tradition involving the consumption of a cocktail shaker full of various kinds of alcohol. Your Dolphins rested at the bottom of the shaker, and you had to drink it all at once and bite the Dolphins in your teeth. You then vomited immediately to avoid alcohol poisoning. The practice is frowned on today.

DRT: Dead reckoning tracker. A table with a glass top and an electric motor that is aligned with the ship's gyrocompass. Allows the navigator to plot the ship's position.

EB: The General Dynamics, Electric Boat Division, in Groton, Connecticut.

EBT: Emergency ballast tank blow.

ECM: Electronics countermeasures.

emergency ballast tank blow: Part of the SUBSAFE system. Normal ballast tank blow procedures are bypassed, and high-pressure air is sent directly into the tanks to bring the submarine to the surface rapidly. You've never felt anything like it.

enlisted head: The toilet for the enlisted men.

ET: An electronics technician.

fairwater planes: Depth-control planes that are located in the submarine's sail. On a 637-class, they were usually operated by the helmsman.

FBMs: Fleet ballistic missile submarines. Also known as SSBNs. The Navy's primary nuclear deterrent. Designed as a mobile missile-launching platform, they can launch as many as sixteen missiles with multiple independent warheads from a submerged location anywhere in the world's oceans.

field day: The entire crew is awake and cleans the submarine from stem to stern. No one is exempt.

fire control party: Members of the watch section delegated to operate the fire control equipment and support the captain in tactical situations.

fish: Torpedoes.

fix: To pinpoint the boat's position at sea.

fleet boats: Diesel-electric-powered submarines.

FT: Fire control technician.

GCT/ARI: Acronym for the general clerical test and the arithmetic test administered to incoming recruits at boot camp.

geedunk: Dessert. Anything sweet.

gilly: the 100% alcohol used to clean electronic equipment.

goat locker: The chief's quarters. The area on a submarine where men with the rank of E-7 or above sleep.

Grinder: In boot camp, it was the parade ground where you marched for hours simply because there was nothing else for you to do. In Connecticut, it is a sandwich made from cold meats and vegetables. In other parts of the country, it is called a submarine sandwich, a sub, or a hero.

gun boss: On a fleet boat, the man responsible for the small arms on board.

guppy II modified: An extensive conversion program that gave fleet boats a snorkel, a more streamlined hull, and a much greater battery capacity.

helmsman: The enlisted man who actually steers the vessel.

ICman: Intercommunications man. The rate responsible for all communications systems on board a submarine.

jerry-rig: Often pronounced jury-rig, it was an improvised solution to a problem. It usually didn't last long.

leading seaman: The head of the deck gang.

LDO: Limited-duty officer. An officer selected for commissioning on the basis of his skill and expertise, and not required to have a Bachelor's degree. In the U.S. Navy, LDOs were former enlisted petty officers or chiefs who were experts in the technical specialty rates from which they came.

lookout "pookah": A small space cut into the sail just behind the slot where the officer of the deck or the captain would stand on the bridge. It helped to protect the lookouts in bad weather.

Mae West: A life preserver that gave you a profile that resembled hers.

mess cook: A galley slave.

midrats: Short for midnight rations. A light meal served at midnight for the ongoing and off-coming watch sections underway. It usually consisted of cold cuts, leftovers, and breakfast pastries.

miss movement: To allow the submarine to leave without you on board. A major no-no!

muster: To count the crew. We often had to.

NATO: North Atlantic Treaty Organization.

Neptune: Roman god of the sea.

Old Man: A euphemism for the Captain.

"one eighty out": A complete turnaround. A reversal of course.

on station: The area where the submarine has been sent to patrol.

on the beach: Ashore. Not on the boat.

OOD: The officer of the deck. The commissioned officer who is supervising the operation of the submarine.

OP: Short for operations. A specific assignment for a submarine.

planesman: The enlisted man responsible for depth control. Usually operates the stern planes or the bow planes.

point Alpha: A point in the ocean south of New London that marked the edge of the continental shelf. Nuclear boats would usually wait until they reached this point to submerge.

polynya: An open area of water that is surrounded by sea ice.

Poseidon: Ancient Greek god of the sea.

PSA: Postshakedown availability. A period in the shipyard when a submarine is available for repairs.

PSI: Pounds per square inch. The measure of any system under pressure.

quartermaster: The enlisted version of a navigator.

quarters: A place where you would sleep. Also an assembling of the crew.

R & R: Rest and recreation. A period when very little work, if any, is done.

race, the: The area of the ocean between the navigational points known as Race Rock and New London Light.

ring knockers: U.S. Naval Academy graduates.

ROTC: Reserve Officer Training Corps. A college campus arm of the military.

scrambled eggs: Gold braid that adorned the bill of an officer's cap. Also a euphemism for officers at the rank of commander or above.

seaman gang, the: Also known as the deck gang, men who had not made rate and who worked directly for the chief of the boat. The COB's personal slaves.

SECNAV: The Secretary of the Navy, an appointment made by the president of the United States, and third in line from the president in the Navy administrative chain of command.

Section 8: A discharge from the U.S. military for reason of being mentally unfit for service, commonly given to service members found guilty of sexual perversion. It was classified as an undesirable discharge that deprived the soldier of veteran's benefits without the loss of any citizenship rights, such as the right to vote. Today, medical discharges for psychological/psychiatric reasons are now covered by a number of regulations.

sextant: A device used to measure the distance from the horizon to a celestial object. Before the gyrocompass, the principal instrument of navigation.

shore patrol: The Navy version of military police.

single up: The lines that tie a submarine to a pier are doubled up. When you single up the lines, it means that you are about to get underway.

skimmers: Any sailor who serves on board a surface ship.

snake ranch: An apartment occupied by one or more bachelor sailors.

snorkeling: The process by which a diesel-electric submarine charges her batteries while remaining submerged.

SONAR: Sound navigation and ranging, sonar is the system by which submarines navigate and detect other vessels. There are two kinds, active and passive. Active uses a transmitter and a receiver. Passive just listens.

SOPA: The senior officer present afloat.

spec ops: Short for special operations. A euphemism for an extended deployment or patrol that usually lasted at least sixty days.

spooks: Sailors who were specialists in electronic intelligence. They usually worked for the National Security Agency and would report on board just before a submarine would leave on patrol. For some reason, they were always disguised as cooks.

squared away: Perfect; according to regulations.

SSBN: Another designation for a fleet ballistic missile submarine.

Steinke hood: Named for its inventor, it was an inflatable life jacket with a hood that completely enclosed the wearer's head, trapping a bubble of breathing air. It was standard equipment on all American submarines during the Cold War.

storekeeper: The guy responsible for all provisions and spare parts on board the boat. A hugely responsible rate on a submarine.

SUBLANT: Commander of Submarine Forces in the Atlantic Fleet.

SUBSAFE: A quality-assurance program designed to guarantee safety on submarines. It was instituted by the Navy after the USS *Thresher* disaster in 1963. No submarine certified by the SUBSAFE program has ever been lost.

surface craft: Anything that isn't a submarine.

Tet Offensive: A military offensive by the North Vietnamese and the Vietcong in January 1968. Coordinated to begin on the Vietnamese Lunar New Year, it lasted for months. Eventually, it was considered a major tactical defeat for the Vietcong and the North Vietnamese. However, in America it had an adverse affect on public opinion and started turning the average person against the war.

three-mile limit: In the 1960s the accepted marker off of the coast of the United States for international waters. The Soviets enforced a twelve-mile limit.

torpedoman: The rate associated with the weapons in the torpedo room. The old joke was "Size 44 jumper, size 2 white hat!"

UQC: An underwater telephone.

VLF loop: An underwater antenna that received regularly scheduled radiow-transmissions.

Wardroom: A room where the commissioned officers eat meals, and where the captain can gather his officers for a meeting.

XO: The executive officer, the second in command. A liaison between the captain and his crew, and the man responsible for discipline on board the boat.

Yankee class: A Soviet missile submarine modeled after the USS *George Washington*.

zig: A turn, or a change in a contact's course.

Sources

Internet

For the reconstruction of all news information:
http://timelines.ws/20thcent/TWENTIETHCENT.HTML (December 31,
2007)

For numbers regarding the development of the Soviet submarine navy:
http://www.time.com/time/magazine/article/0,9171,837933-1,00.html
(December 31, 2007)

For the history of the USS *Sturgeon*:
http://www.navyhistory.com/Submarine/SturgeonIII.html (December 31,
2007)

For information about SUBROC:
http://americanhistory.si.edu/subs/weapons/armament/other/index.html
(December 31, 2007)

For weather information:
http://www.zetnet.co.uk/sigs/weather/Met_Codes/beaufort.htm (December
31, 2007)

For general submarine information:

http://www.submarinesailor.com/default.asp (December 31, 2007)

http://navysite.de/crew.php?action=ship&ship=ssn_637 (December 31, 2007)

http://www.globalsecurity.org/military/systems/ship/ssn-637.htm (December 31, 2007)

For victor-class submarines:

http://www.globalsecurity.org/military/world/russia/671.htm (December 31, 2007)

For the USS *Dogfish*:

http://www.ussdogfish.com/index.html (December 31, 2007)

For Kent State:

http://www.may4.org/?q=node/5 (December 31, 2007)

For IQ:

http://wilderdom.com/intelligence/IQWhatScoresMean.html (December 31, 2007)

http://cps.nova.edu/~cpphelp/WAIS-R.html (December 31, 2007)

For alcohol consumption:

http://www.alcoholisminformation.com/How_Much_Alcohol_Is_In_One_Shot_Glass.html (December 31, 2007)

For the UCMJ:

http://usmilitary.about.com/od/punitivearticles/a/mcm112a.htm (December 31, 2007)

For the USS *Squalus*:

http://www.onr.navy.mil/focus/blowballast/squalus/default.htm (December 31, 2007)

On submarine pay:

http://larryshomeport.com/html/subpay.html (December 31, 2007)

http://www.nps.gov/sahi/supportyourpark/upload/2005-mayJune.pdf
    (December 31, 2007)

http://www.geocities.com/gwmccue/Documents/Roosevelt.html (December
    31, 2007)

For the Steinke Hood:

http://www.globalsecurity.org/military/systems/ship/systems/steinke-hood
    .htm (December 31, 2007)

Publications

Blind Man's Bluff, The Untold Story of American Submarine Espionage,
    Sherry Sontag and Christopher Drew, Public Affairs, 1998

Silent Steel, The Mysterious Death of the Nuclear Attack Sub SCORPION,
    Stephen Johnson, John Wiley & Sons, 2006

Index

About the Author

GANNON MCHALE is a New York–based character actor. Over the past thirty years he has enjoyed a modest journeyman's career that includes shows on Broadway, Off-Broadway, in regional theatres, and on tours across North America, Europe, and Asia. He has appeared on stage in forty-five of the fifty states, including Alaska and Hawaii; all of the western provincial capitals of Canada; four countries in Europe; and two countries in Asia, including a twenty-nine-city tour of Japan that was the cultural experience of a lifetime. A proud member of the Actor's Equity Association, he is also a life member of the U.S. Submarine Veterans Association and the International Submariner's Association.

The Naval Institute Press is the book-publishing arm of the U.S. Naval Institute, a private, nonprofit, membership society for sea service professionals and others who share an interest in naval and maritime affairs. Established in 1873 at the U.S. Naval Academy in Annapolis, Maryland, where its offices remain today, the Naval Institute has members worldwide.

Members of the Naval Institute support the education programs of the society and receive the influential monthly magazine *Proceedings* or the colorful bimonthly magazine *Naval History* and discounts on fine nautical prints and on ship and aircraft photos. They also have access to the transcripts of the Institute's Oral History Program and get discounted admission to any of the Institute-sponsored seminars offered around the country.

The Naval Institute's book-publishing program, begun in 1898 with basic guides to naval practices, has broadened its scope to include books of more general interest. Now the Naval Institute Press publishes about seventy titles each year, ranging from how-to books on boating and navigation to battle histories, biographies, ship and aircraft guides, and novels. Institute members receive significant discounts on the Press's more than eight hundred books in print.

Full-time students are eligible for special half-price membership rates. Life memberships are also available.

For a free catalog describing Naval Institute Press books currently available, and for further information about joining the U.S. Naval Institute, please write to:

Member Services
U.S. Naval Institute
291 Wood Road
Annapolis, MD 21402-5034
Telephone: (800) 233-8764
Fax: (410) 571-1703
Web address: www.usni.org